Fortress • 68

American Civil War Fortifications (3)

The Mississippi and River Forts

Ron Field • Illustrated by Adam Hook

Series editors Marcus Cowper and Nikolai Bogdanovic

First published in 2007 by Osprey Publishing
Midland House, West Way, Botley, Oxford OX2 0PH, UK
443 Park Avenue South, New York, NY 10016, USA
E-mail: info@ospreypublishing.com

ISBN 978 184603 194 6

Editorial by Ilios Publishing, Oxford, UK (www.iliospublishing.com)
Cartography by The Map Studio, Romsey, UK
Design by Ken Vail Graphic Design, Cambridge, UK
Typeset in Monotype Gill Sans and ITC Stone Serif
Index by Alan Thatcher
Originated by PDQ Media, Bungay, UK
Printed in China through Bookbuilders

07 08 09   10 9 8 7 6 5 4 3 2 1

A CIP catalog record for this book is available from the British Library.

FOR A CATALOG OF ALL BOOKS PUBLISHED BY OSPREY MILITARY AND AVIATION
PLEASE CONTACT:

Osprey Direct, c/o Random House Distribution Center, 400 Hahn Road, Westminster,
MD 21157
Email: info@ospreydirect.com

Osprey Direct UK, P.O. Box 140, Wellingborough, Northants, NN8 2FA, UK
E-mail: info@ospreydirect.co.uk

www.ospreypublishing.com

Acknowledgments

The author would like to express his thanks to: Edwin C. Bearss,
Civil War Preservation Trust Trustee and Chief Historian Emeritus
of the US National Park Service; Terrence J. Winschel, Historian;
Virginia S. DuBowy, Park Guide, Vicksburg National Military Park;
Charis Wilson, Records Manager/FOIA Officer, National Park
Service – DSC, Technical Information Center, Denver, CO; Clifton
Hyatt, Curator of Photography, US Army Military History Institute
Carlisle Barracks, PA; Renée Klish, Army Art Curator, US Army
Center of Military History, Washington, DC; Cynthia Luckie,
Curator of Photographs, and Meredith McLemore, Archivist,
Alabama Department of Archives & History.

Artist's note

Readers may care to note that the original paintings from which
the color plates in this book were prepared are available for
private sale. All reproduction copyright whatsoever is retained by
the Publishers. All inquiries should be addressed to:

Scorpio Gallery
PO Box 475
Hailsham
East Sussex
BN27 2SL
UK

The Publishers regret that they can enter into no correspondence
upon this matter.

The Fortress Study Group (FSG)

The object of the FSG is to advance the education of the public in
the study of all aspects of fortifications and their armaments,
especially works constructed to mount or resist artillery. The FSG
holds an annual conference in September over a long weekend
with visits and evening lectures, an annual tour abroad lasting
about eight days, and an annual Members' Day.
The FSG journal FORT is published annually, and its newsletter
Casemate is published three times a year. Membership is
international. For further details, please contact:

The Secretary, c/o 6 Lanark Place, London W9 1BS, UK
Website: www.fsgfort.com

Front cover
The Siege of Vicksburg, by Kurz & Allison, Art Publishers, Chicago,
USA, 1888. (Library of Congress: LC-USZC4-1754)

Contents

Introduction

The Mississippi River played a decisive role in the American Civil War, and mastery of this major artery, and its tributaries, was recognized by both Union and Confederate authorities as the major factor in any strategy for winning the war in the West. Not only would control of this mighty river provide a means for the movement of troops and war materials, it also offered access to world markets for industrial and agricultural products for both the North or the South. The lower river valley was bounded for hundreds of miles on its east side from Kentucky through Tennessee and Mississippi by a line of high bluffs and ridges. As the river wound southward towards Louisiana through its lower basin, it occasionally looped against the base of this escarpment at places such as Columbus, the First and Second Chickasaw Bluffs, Memphis, Vicksburg, Grand Gulf, and Port Hudson. With only a small navy, the Confederacy had to rely on fortifications to maintain its hold on the Mississippi River.

Hence they concentrated their forces in earthworks on the numerous high bluffs overlooking the river. These were virtually unassailable to foot soldiers, while naval guns on river-borne warships could not elevate high enough to fire on them. Meanwhile, the defenders found it easier to rain down an effective fire from above.

The Confederate fortifications that controlled the lower Mississippi Valley were put to the test in the lengthy Federal campaign of 1862–63, which was based on the "Anaconda Plan" devised in 1861 by General-in-Chief Winfield Scott. Aimed at strangling the South into submission via a naval blockade at sea and the capture of the entire length of the Mississippi River using a fleet of gunboats supported by the army, this plan would also cut off the Confederate states of Arkansas, western Louisiana and Texas and block the vital trade route from Matamoras, Mexico, which crossed the Mississippi at Vicksburg, and ran via railroad to Richmond, Virginia.

Vicksburg became a fortress city. Known as the "Gibraltar of the Confederacy," its capture was seen by President Abraham Lincoln as "the key" to Union victory in the war. Standing high above the east bank of the Mississippi about 300 miles from the river exit into the Gulf of Mexico, and surrounded by difficult terrain for any attacking force, it presented a formidable obstacle to the forces of General Ulysses S. Grant in 1863. Its defenses boasted a network of fortifications, including the Stockade Redan, the Great Redoubt, and the Second Texas Lunette. The initial Federal attacks on May 19 and 22, 1863 failed to breach these defenses and take the city, and a state of siege ensued which saw the creation of a complex system of trenches, tunnels, mines, and batteries to invest the place. As the siege wore on, the conditions for the defenders worsened and Confederate forces, amounting to approximately 29,500, finally surrendered on July 4, 1863. Nearly 3,500 were killed or wounded in both armies during the 47-day siege. Combined with Lee's failure to break through the Union lines on Cemetery Ridge at Gettysburg the day before, the Federal capture of Vicksburg was seen as a defining moment that led to the ultimate triumph of the Union in 1865. With the fall of Port Hudson five days later, Federal forces were in control of the entire length of the Mississippi

The commercial publisher J. B. Elliott of Cincinnati published a cartoon map in 1861 entitled "Scott's Great Snake" which illustrated General Winfield Scott's plan to crush the South both economically and militarily. The plan called for a strong blockade of the Southern ports and a major offensive down the Mississippi River to divide the South. The press ridiculed this as the "Anaconda Plan," but this general scheme contributed greatly to the Northern victory in 1865. (Library of Congress)

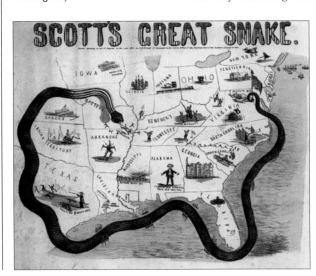

Winfield Scott

Winfield Scott was born in Virginia in 1786 and became a captain in the US Army in 1808. He served on the Niagara front in the War of 1812 and was promoted to brigadier general in 1814. He supervised the preparation of the army's first standard drill regulations in 1815, and visited Europe to study French military methods. He commanded field forces in the Black Hawk War of 1832, and the Second Seminole and Creek Wars of 1836, and was promoted to major general in June 1841. He served as commanding general of the US Army from 1841 to 1861, and led American forces in the decisive campaign of the Mexican War from the Vera Cruz landings to the capture of Mexico City in 1847.

Too old to take a field command at the outbreak of the Civil War in 1861, Scott advised his protégé, Major General George Brinton McClellan, that he believed an effective naval blockade of Southern ports and a strong thrust down the Mississippi Valley with a large force, would isolate the Confederacy and "bring it to terms." Contemporary accounts suggest that McClellan dubbed it Scott's "boa-constrictor" plan. Presenting it to President Abraham Lincoln in greater detail, Scott proposed that 60,000 troops accompanied by gunboats advance down the Mississippi until they had secured the river from Cairo, Illinois, to the Gulf of Mexico. In concert with an effective blockade, he believed this would seal off the South. He further recommended that Federal operations should halt and wait for Southern Union sympathizers to compel their Confederate governors to surrender. It was his conviction that sympathy for secession was not as strong as it appeared, and that isolation would make the Southern "fire-eaters" back down and allow calmer heads to prevail. But Northern radicals wanted combat not armed diplomacy, and the passive features of Scott's plan were disregarded as impractical. Recalling McClellan's alleged "boa-constrictor" remark, the Northern press named the plan for a different constricting snake, the anaconda. Though not adopted at that time, a more aggressive version of the plan was realized during the Western river operations conducted by Grant and Banks in conjunction with the navy during 1862–63. Meanwhile, Scott retired from active service in November 1861, and died at West Point, New York, in 1866. (Painting by Giuseppina Vannutelli, US Army Art Collection)

The Anaconda Plan was on its way to realization and Lincoln wrote on August 26, 1863: "The Father of Waters again goes unvexed to the sea."

Following the capture of Vicksburg, the Federals repaired the old Confederate defenses and constructed their own line of fortifications, the whole complex being known as Fort Grant. Although Vicksburg is the best-known site in the Western theater of the Civil War, numerous other fortified strongholds were established by both armies along Mid-Western rivers such as the Mississippi, Tennessee, and Cumberland. These included Forts Henry and Donelson, Island No. 10, and Fort Pemberton. Most of these forts were protected by earthen parapets reinforced by logs. Although a post constructed of brick or stone might have provided more permanence, earthen walls could be built and repaired more quickly by the Confederate engineers. Armed with heavy guns and manned by small permanent garrisons, some of these forts assumed the importance of permanent fortifications containing much larger bodies of troops during the campaigns of Grant and Banks. In order to capture all of these stronger places, the Union army had to employ regular siege warfare.

Produced in New York during 1863 by Currier & Ives, this lithograph shows Admiral Porter's fleet running the Confederate blockade of the Mississippi River at Vicksburg on April 16, 1863. (Library of Congress: LC-USZC2-1917)

Chronology

1861   April: Confederates establish Fort Wright, Tennessee.

May: Federals fortify St. Louis, Missouri.

May: Fort Prentiss (later Camp Defiance) established at Cairo.

May: Federals fortify Bird's Point, Missouri.

May: Confederate fortifications begun at Forts Henry and Donelson, Tennessee.

June: Confederates fortify Memphis.

June 6: Confederates establish Fort Cleburne/Pillow in Tennessee.

July: Fort Girardeau established at Girardeau, Missouri.

July: Confederate fortifications started at New Madrid, Missouri.

August: Confederate fortifications begun at Island No. 10.

August: city defenses under construction at New Orleans.

1862   February 6, 12–16: Grant captures Forts Henry and Donelson.

March 13: McCown evacuates New Madrid.

March 21: fortifications begun at Vicksburg.

April 7: Mackall surrenders Island No. 10 to Grant.

April 29: New Orleans surrenders.

June: Confederates evacuate Forts Pillow and Harris.

August: Port Hudson fortified.

1863   January 10–11: Fort Hindman/Arkansas Post established.

March 11: Confederates hold back Federal advance at Fort Pemberton.

March 31–April 1: Forts Wade and Cobun captured.

May 18–19, 22: Grant's army unsuccessfully assaults Vicksburg defenses.

May 22: siege of Vicksburg begins.

July 4: siege of Vicksburg ends with Confederate surrender.

July 9: Port Hudson falls. The Federals now control the Mississippi River.

Federal troops behind flying saps fire on the Third Louisiana Redan shortly after the mine was blown on June 25, 1863. Note the reserves in the trenches to their rear, and the 45th Illinois Infantry advancing into the crater. (Author's collection)

The river campaigns, 1861–64

The down-river campaign

St. Louis, 1861–63

St. Louis in Missouri played a key role as a strategic staging ground for the Union army during the war in the west, and served as headquarters of the Western Department in 1861. Located in the city were major training camps at Benton Barracks, Fort Ruedi, Camp Cavender, and Schofield Barracks. As early as May 1861, the Southern press recorded that the city was "environed by a line of military posts, extending from the river below the arsenal, around the western outskirts, to the river again on the north." By the fall of the year, a system of earthen forts had indeed been constructed around the area. On October 14, 1861, the *Daily Dispatch*, published in the Confederate capital of Richmond, Virginia, reported:

> The whole city of St. Louis, on every side save the river, is well fortified with heavy earthwork defences, surmounted by huge columbiads, rifled guns and howitzers. There are guns on redoubts, guns on boats, guns at the arsenal, guns at the various departments – in fact guns everywhere.

Little is known of these fortifications. Fort No. 1 was built by a Missouri Pioneer Company commanded by Captain Alfred H. Piquenard. Fort No. 3, containing a star fort or cruciform-shaped redoubt, was located north of Salena and Lynch streets in the Benton Park area, the remains of which survived until the 1870s.

Cape Girardeau, 1861–63

The first high ground north of the confluence of the Ohio and Mississippi rivers, Cape Girardeau, in southeastern Missouri, provided a strategic position from which Federal guns could fire on approaching Confederate gunboats. Hence in July 1861, Major General John C. Fremont, commanding the Department of the West, ordered the 20th Illinois Infantry, under Colonel C. Carroll Marsh, to occupy that place, and it remained under Union control throughout the war.

A bird's-eye view of St. Louis, Missouri, produced in 1859 by A. Janicke & Co., which shows the bustling levee with numerous steamboats at anchor. This city would become a major staging ground for Grant's river campaigns and served as headquarters of the Western Department in 1861. (Library of Congress LC-USZC2-1740)

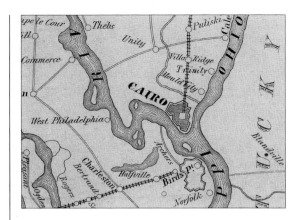

Cairo quickly became a large Federal military encampment for most of the Illinois regiments in the early years of the war. Grant expanded Fort Prentiss into the new and massive Fort Defiance, which served as a staging area for forays into Missouri and, later, down the Mississippi River. Depicted in the upper right *Harper's Weekly* engraving based on a sketch by Alexander Simplot, the Ohio levee became the site of a US Navy base, which hosted both commercial wharf boats carrying supplies and navy gunboats. (Library of Congress/author's collection)

To protect the city from both the land and river approaches, Major Ignatz G. Kappner, of the Engineer Department of the West, was ordered there with Companies A, B and G, Engineer Regiment of the West, to build four forts and two batteries. Named Forts A, B, C, D, and Batteries A and B, they were known collectively as Fort Girardeau. The four forts formed a crescent along the outskirts of the town. Consisting of a triangular-shaped earthwork with a palisade on the side facing the river, plus 24- and 32-pounder cannon emplacements and rifle pits, Fort D was the most heavily armed fort, and the only one not dismantled after the war. Located at the corner of Locust and Fort streets, the site is now part of a three-acre city park. Fort A incorporated a grist mill, and was located at the east end of Bellevue Street. Fort B was built near the Dittlinger House on Academic Hill, located on the grounds of present-day Southeast Missouri State University. Fort C was at the end of Ellis Street at Good Hope and Sprigg streets, and is commemorated by a stone monument. Battery A, of two guns, was located north of Fort B, at Henderson and New Madrid streets. Battery B, of four guns, was placed on Thilenius Hill.

Cairo and Bird's Point, 1861

At the fork of the Mississippi and Ohio rivers, the township of Cairo was considered of great strategic importance in Union plans to use the river route to invade the South. Hence, fortifications called Fort Prentiss were under way as soon as the Union army occupied that place. On June 24, 1861 the Cairo correspondent of the *Chicago Times* wrote:

> A large force has been engaged during the past few days tearing down buildings at the extreme point, to make way for the proposed fortifications. A heavy construction train is bringing in earth from a point twelve miles out, on the line of the [Illinois] Central railroad, to construct a cross embankment from the Ohio to the Mississippi levee, so as to enclose an area of about six acres. When this embankment is finished as laid out, the troops here will be amply protected on every side by breastworks of a character that would resist the heaviest cannonading for perhaps a twelve month.

By the end of June, *Harper's Weekly* reported: "There are now about 8,000 men in and about Cairo and Bird's Point. Some 3,000 are in barracks at the Point [at Cairo], which has been named Camp Defiance, and latterly have been busily employed in removing obstructions and erecting substantial fortifications." By the end of July 1861, Camp Defiance had been re-named Fort Prentiss, for Colonel Benjamin M. Prentiss, 10th Illinois Infantry, and contained "One 64-pounder, three 24-pounders, and three 32-pounders, and any amount of small guns and flying artillery." A correspondent of the Memphis *Daily Appeal* concluded that the "breastworks are impregnable."

Another fortified encampment called Camp Smith was established north of the city. One battery of heavy artillery was placed on the extreme southern point of the levee, while four light batteries protected the water front either side and were under orders to fire on any vessel which refused to heave to and be searched. According to a report for the Cincinnati *Enquirer* dated July 15, 1861, the completed breastworks at Cairo were "nine feet wide at the summit and twenty feet at the base; hight [sic] seven feet, with bench two feet high inside for the men to stand on, with a ditch … of a depth of ten feet and a width of twelve feet, and is built on [Confederate] Gen. Pillow's plan, although not his side of the entrenchment."

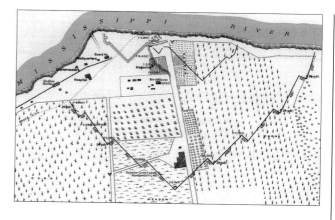

Across the Mississippi River from Cairo, Bird's Point was occupied and fortified by Federal troops to prevent Confederate forces in Missouri from shelling Fort Defiance. *(Official Military Atlas of the Civil War)*

According to a report in the Memphis *Daily Appeal* in early June 1861, the fortifications across the river at Bird's Point consisted of "a ditch four feet deep and five feet wide and four hundred feet in length, making the embankment about nine feet high. The approaches to either end of the ditch will be defended by cannon." By late summer these fortifications had expanded to include much longer outer earthworks containing five 24-pounders protecting a magazine, headquarters building, hospital, guardhouse and quartermaster stores.

New Madrid

The first line of Confederate defense in the Mississippi River valley was established by General Gideon Pillow, commanding the newly formed "Army of Liberation," at New Madrid, Missouri in July 1861. This was to be the base for future expeditions up river, both by land and water. Chosen for several reasons, New Madrid was the terminus of the main river road leading to St. Louis, which was 175 miles to the north. The town was also located at the top of the second of two horseshoe bends of the river, which formed sweeping arcs, appearing on the map like the letter "S" laid on its side. Up river from New Madrid was Island No. 10, situated in the middle of the Mississippi, which could be easily fortified to block the passage of Federal gunboats. Captain Andrew Belcher Gray, of the CS Provisional Engineers, reported on August 14, 1861 that this island was "a strong position naturally for erecting works to defend the passage of the Mississippi River," but Pillow had different ideas. A political general from Tennessee, his first object was an invasion of Missouri, which became bogged down when he attempted to join forces with General William J. Hardee. Meanwhile, the construction of fortifications was ignored and his army sat idle.

The following month Kentucky became the new object of the Confederate commander's attention and Pillow reported to General Leonidas Polk in Memphis that the strategic value of Island No. 10 was "vastly overrated." A West Point graduate who had spent most of the past 20 years in the ministry, Polk depended on Pillow's judgment. The two agreed that the high bluffs at Columbus, Kentucky, were better for defense, and the army moved into Kentucky on September 3, 1861. This created a political backlash, as that state had proclaimed its neutrality to both sides on May 20 of that year.

Pillow's advance into Kentucky left the few fortifications begun in New Madrid unfinished, leaving their completion to Brigadier General M. Jeff Thompson and his contingent of the Missouri State Guard. Those at Island No. 10 were completely abandoned. However, after Polk moved his headquarters up to Columbus he directed the works at New Madrid and Island No. 10 to be finished off, recognizing the importance of maintaining a fall-back position from the Kentucky fortress. By early December 1861, the forces under General Thompson had under construction Fort Thompson, a small redoubt with a bastion at each of

The forts of the Mississippi River and its tributaries.

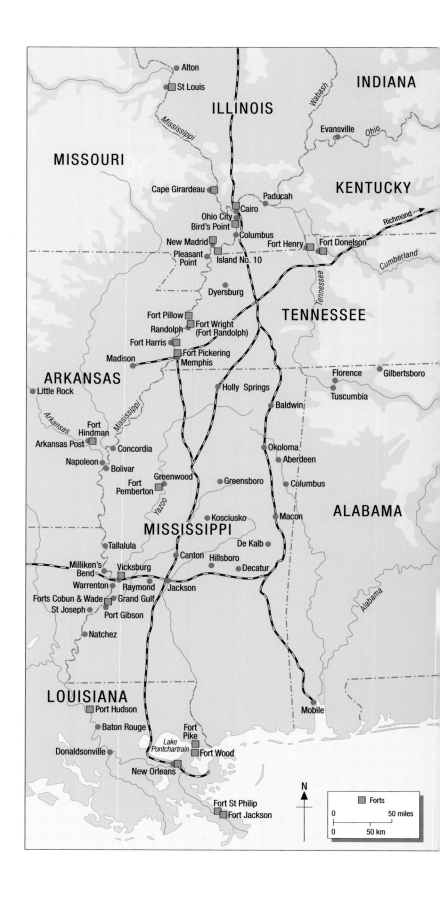

Alton
St Louis

ILLINOIS

Wabash

INDIANA

MISSOURI

Mississippi

Evansville
Ohio

KENTUCKY

Cape Girardeau
Paducah

Cairo
Ohio City
Bird's Point
New Madrid
Columbus
Fort Henry
Fort Donelson
Richmond

Pleasant
Point
Island No. 10
Cumberland

Dyersburg

Tennessee

Fort Pillow
Fort Wright
(Fort Randolph)
Randolph
Fort Harris
Fort Pickering
Madison
Memphis

TENNESSEE

Florence
Gilbertsboro
Tuscumbia

ARKANSAS

Little Rock

Holly Springs

Baldwin

Arkansas

Mississippi

Fort
Hindman
Arkansas Post
Concordia
Napoleon
Bolivar

Okoloma
Aberdeen

Greenwood
Fort
Pemberton

Greensboro
Columbus

Yazoo

MISSISSIPPI

Kosciusko

Macon

ALABAMA

Tallalula

De Kalb

Milliken's
Bend
Vicksburg
Canton
Hillsboro
Decatur

Warrenton
Raymond
Jackson
Forts Cobun & Wade
Grand Gulf
St Joseph
Port Gibson

Alabama

Natchez

LOUISIANA
Port Hudson

Mobile

Baton Rouge
Fort
Pike

Donaldsonville
Lake
Pontchartrain
Fort Wood

New Orleans

Fort St Philip
Fort Jackson

N

Forts

0   50 miles

0   50 km

its four corners, situated about one mile to the west of New Madrid. Garrisoned by the 11th and 12th Arkansas, under Colonel Edward W. Gantt, this fort eventually held fourteen 24- and 48-pounder cannon.

Immediately to the east of the city, Fort Bankhead (a.k.a. Fort Madrid), with a breastwork composed of sacks of shelled corn covered with dirt, was constructed by the 1st Alabama, Tennessee & Mississippi (a.k.a. 4th Confederate) by February/March 1862. According to the report of General Alexander P. "Old Straight" Stewart, who assumed command of Confederate forces at New Madrid on February 26, this fort had "a strong parapet ditch, and beyond the latter a sort of abatis of brush and felled trees. It was an irregular line, extending from the [St. John] bayou above the town to the river, some 300 or 400 yards below." Named for Captain Smith P. Bankhead, whose six light guns of Co. B, Tennessee Artillery Corps, were placed on platforms behind the parapet, these works also contained four smooth-bore 32-pounders.

Forts Henry and Donelson, 1861–62

Having seized Paducah, Kentucky, which controlled access to the Tennessee and Cumberland, on September 6, 1861, Grant began operations down those rivers using gunboats designed specifically for joint operations with the Union army. The seizure of Fort Henry, on the Tennessee, and Fort Donelson, on the Cumberland, would open routes for invasion and turn the flanks of Confederate forces at Columbus and Bowling Green, Kentucky.

Described by J. F. Gilmer, Lieutenant Colonel of Engineers and Chief Engineer Western Department, as "a strong field work of fine bastion front," Fort Henry was an irregular convex polygon redoubt accessed via a drawbridge in its southwest curtain wall, with four redans, or outward projecting angles, begun in 1861 under the direction of engineer officer Lieutenant Joseph Dixon, who was later killed during the bombardment of Fort Donelson. According to Gilmer, the guns at Fort Henry were mounted on "substantial wooden platforms," and consisted of "one 10-inch columbiad [on an all-iron carriage on all-iron chassis], one rifled gun of 24-pounder caliber (weight of ball 62 pounds), two 42-pounders, and eight 32-pounders, all arranged to fire through embrasures formed by raising the parapet between the guns with sand bags carefully laid." This armament was later supplemented by two more 32-pounders and two 12-pounders.

Standing in low ground on the east bank of the Tennessee River, Fort Henry was also protected by rifle trenches to the east and southeast, and abatis, or sharpened tree branches, pointing toward the enemy. It was also planned to place cannon on several of the hilltops overlooking the fort from the opposite river bank, but this was not done due to the lack of a labor force and a shortage of artillery pieces.

The fort was partially flooded on February 6, 1862 – the day of the Federal naval attack. The defenders consisted of only 100 artillerymen, as Brigadier General Lloyd Tilghman had ordered the rest of the garrison to Fort Donelson. Standing on higher ground and named for the German immigrant commander of the 10th Tennessee Infantry, Fort Heiman was designed to protect Fort Donelson, but was also unfinished at that time. After a short bombardment by Flag Officer Andrew H. Foote's seven ironclad river gunboats, General Tilghman surrendered with 80 surviving artillerymen. Occupied by Federal forces, Fort Henry was renamed Fort Foote, for the naval commander mainly responsible for its capture. Consisting of a division of three brigades under General C. F. Smith and a division of two brigades under General John A. McClernand, Grant's land forces, which had been delayed by weather and muddy roads, were not needed for the assault.

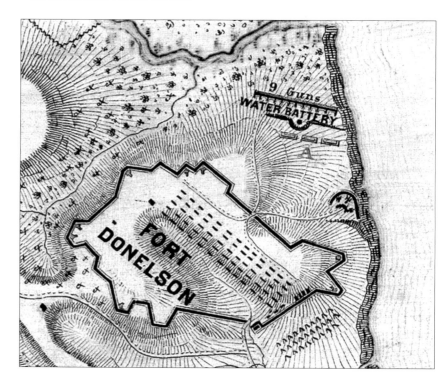

Detail from a map showing Fort Donelson and its nine-gun water battery on the Cumberland River, drawn by Lieutenant Otto H. Matz, Assistant Topographical Engineer, under the supervision of Lieutenant Colonel J. B. McPherson, chief engineer on the staff of General Grant. (Library of Congress)

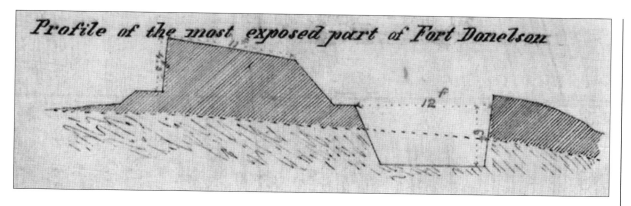

Fort Heiman was later re-occupied by Confederate forces under Nathan Bedford Forrest. Using masked batteries, he ambushed Federal vessels including the *Mazeppa*, which was sunk on October 29, 1864. Forrest also used the fort as a base of operations from which to raid the Federal supply depot at Johnsonville, some 30 miles to the south on the east bank of the Tennessee River.

With the capture of Fort Henry, Grant started overland for Fort Donelson, which he reached on February 11, 1862. According to General Pillow, the selection of the site for Fort Donelson was "an unfortunate one." While it controlled the river, he reported on February 18:

> The site was commanded by the heights above and below on the river and by a continuous range of hills all around the works to its rear. A field work of very contracted dimensions had been constructed by the garrison to protect the battery; but the field works were commanded by the hills already referred to, and lay open to a fire of artillery from every direction except from the hills below.

Two members of the Engineer Corps, Provisional Army of Tennessee, William F. Foster and Adna Anderson, were ordered on May 10, 1861, to find suitable ground just inside the Tennessee border to simultaneously cover both the Tennessee and Cumberland. They then focused on surveying possible sites along the Cumberland River, looking at the high ridges and deep hollows near the Kentucky border. In mid-May, on the west bank of the river not far below the town of Dover, Anderson laid out the water battery of Fort Donelson 12 miles from the Kentucky state line. The new fort was named in honor of Brigadier General Daniel S. Donelson, adjutant general of the Army of Tennessee, who, with Colonel Bushrod Johnson of the Corps of Engineers, approved of the site. Construction was begun by a large force of men brought from the nearby Cumberland Iron Works.

Later constructed under the supervision of Lieutenant Joseph Dixon, CS Army, the main earthworks at Fort Donelson consisted of a 15-acre fortress, which included at least 10 redans. Outer field works, including at least seven more redans plus extensive trenches and rifle pits, protected the western and southern approaches, while a backwater "impassable except by boats and bridges" formed an obstacle from the north. The earthen parapet around the main works was about 20ft wide at its base and

This profile of the weakest part of the defenses at Fort Donelson, Tennessee, indicates that the parapet was only about 6ft high in places and 15ft wide. (Library of Congress)

Federal troops of Brigadier General Charles F. Smith's division break through the earthwork parapet of Fort Donelson, Tennessee, on July 16, 1863, after the inept command of Confederate General John Floyd left the western end of the fort defended by a single regiment. Fort Donelson was surrendered "unconditionally" shortly after this action. (Author's collection)

Fort Henry

Standing in low ground on the east bank of the Tennessee River, Fort Henry was an irregular convex polygon redoubt containing 17 guns of varying caliber when attacked and captured by Federal forces on February 6, 1862. Each of the guns was mounted behind sandbagged embrasures. The 15ft-wide earthen parapets were fronted by a 9ft-deep and 20ft-wide ditch, which was partially flooded. Access was gained via a drawbridge in the south west curtain wall (**1**). Officers' quarters were wood framed with pitched shingle roofs (**2**). The men's quarters, or barracks, were log structures with pitched roofs (**3**). The ordnance store was a log structure with a lean-to sloping roof covered with earth (**4**). Additional accommodation was provided by tents of various sizes, but mainly two-man shelter tents (**5**). A stockade ran from the point of the northwest redan or bastion to the river (**6**). Protection was also afforded by rifle trenches to the east and southeast, and abatis, or sharpened tree branches pointing toward the enemy, on all sides.

The drawbridge mechanism (**7a** plan view, and **7b** section) probably consisted of "a light rolling bridge" of the type designed by Colonel Bergère of the French engineers, composed of a wooden platform spanning the ditch, with levers weighted at the end by shells filled with sand or shot, attached to two ordinary gun carriage wheels which ran backwards along rails. This was operated by taking hold of the wheel spokes and raising or lowering the bridge by rolling the wheels either forwards or backwards along the rails.

Part of the original earthwork parapet at Fort Donelson stands out clearly in this photograph taken in June 2006. (Photograph courtesy of Niki Conolly)

approximately 12ft high, with a 6ft-deep ditch surrounding it. All the trees around the fort for over 200 yards' distance were felled to provide clear fields of fire and observation, and the approaches were protected by abatis and trous-de-loup. The lower water battery contained eight 32-pounder guns on barbette carriages, plus one 10in. Columbiad. The upper water battery held two 32-pounder carronades and one 32-pounder rifle gun. A total of 67 guns were found in the works when the fort was captured.

On February 16, 1862, after the mismanagement of command between Confederate generals Floyd, Buckner, and Pillow, and the failure of an all-out Confederate attack aimed at breaking through Grant's lines of investment to the south, the fort's 12,000-man garrison under General Simon Bolivar Buckner surrendered unconditionally. This was a major victory for Grant and a catastrophe for the South. It ensured that Kentucky would remain in the Union and opened up Tennessee for a Northern advance down the Tennessee and Cumberland rivers. Grant received a promotion to major general for his victory and attained growing stature in the Western theater of war, earning the *nom de guerre* "Unconditional Surrender."

Island No. 10, 1861–62

Following the fall of Forts Henry and Donelson, the first line of Confederate defense of the Mississippi Valley was breached, and Columbus was now vulnerable to an overland attack from the east. Polk quickly moved his headquarters to Humboldt, Tennessee and ordered a division from Columbus

Fort Henry

7b

7a

15

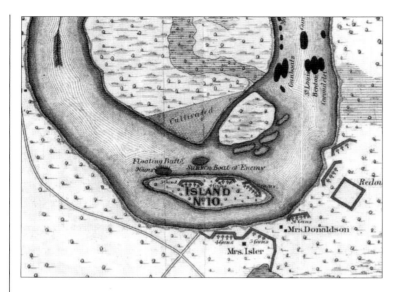

Published in 1866 to accompany the report of Major General John Pope to the Committee on the Conduct of the War, this rather fanciful map of Island No. 10 shows the redans and redoubt called Fort Leonidas on the Tennessee shore, the batteries on the island itself, plus the floating battery *New Orleans*. (Rucker Agee Map Collection, Birmingham Public Library, Birmingham)

to New Madrid and Island No. 10. Brigadier General John P. McCown, a Tennessee West Point graduate and former captain in the US regulars, was placed in command of these forces.

On November 22, 1861 Captain Gray, of the Provisional Engineers, had been tasked with the completion of a series of land batteries on and near Island No. 10 using local slave labor. He worked tirelessly on these defenses throughout the winter months. Large seacoast artillery was shipped down from Columbus, and by mid-March 1862, 52 guns had been mounted on and around the island. Of the seven batteries on the Tennessee shore, the northernmost was called the Redan Battery. Commanded by Captain Edward W. Rucker, CS Army, it was armed with three 8in. Columbiads and three 32-pounders (smoothbore). According to Gray, the parapet in this redan was "much weakened by embrasures, made necessary by the 32-pounders being mounted upon naval carriages or trucks." This fort was also partially flooded when three Federal ironclads under Flag Officer Foote attacked on March 13, 1862.

Standing at the rear of the nearby Confederate batteries on the Tennessee shore was Fort Leonidas, a four-sided redoubt. There were also four batteries on the island itself, the largest of which was named Island Battery No. 1, and contained the massive "Lady Polk, Jr." – a 128-pounder rifled gun. These were augmented by the floating battery *New Orleans*, which mounted one rifled 32-pounder and eight 8in. columbiads, and was moored off the northwest end of the Island. Originally designed as a dry dock rather than a ship at Algiers (across the river from New Orleans) during the fall of 1861, the floating battery had a unique defensive system. A pumping engine in the hold allowed the crew to lower it until the deck was flush with the water. Although this protected New Orleans from the relatively flat trajectories of naval guns, it was unprotected from the plunging shots of mortars.

With the commencement of the main Federal bombardment on March 13, 1862, McCown ordered the evacuation of New Madrid and moved his garrison across the river to the peninsula in order to avoid being surrounded by the forces of General John Pope. Due to his mismanagement of this operation, McCown was relieved of command and replaced by General W. W. Mackall. Meanwhile, Pope ordered a canal cut through the swamps so that his boats could by-pass the defenses of Island No. 10. After its completion by April 4, he ferried four regiments over the river south of New Madrid three days later, which effectively cut off the Confederate line of retreat at Tiptonville. Mackall subsequently surrendered 3,500 men, while 500 escaped through the swamps. The Federal victory opened the Mississippi River to Fort Pillow, about 40 miles above Memphis, and gave Pope a reputation which led to his appointment as commander of the Army of Virginia two months later.

Fort Pillow, 1861–64

According to a report published by the New York *Tribune* after the Federal occupation of Fort Pillow in June 1862, the location of that post on the Mississippi River was "most favorable for defense. The river at Craighead Point makes a very sudden bend, running nearly north and south, and narrowing so remarkably that at the lower end of the works it is not more than half a mile wide, and at their first batteries is about three-quarters of a mile; bringing all boats within easy range of their guns, and rendering their escape almost an impossibility."

These Confederate fortifications began as a smaller post called Fort Cleburne when a small force of Arkansas volunteers under Colonel Patrick Cleburne probed about 12 miles upstream from Fort Wright on June 6, 1861 to construct an advanced "post of honor" on the high First Chickasaw Bluffs. Following the acceptance of Tennessee forces into Confederate service at the beginning of July 1861, General Pillow decided to expand Cleburne's battery into a huge fortification, and ordered to the post from Fort Randolph Captain Montgomery Lynch, CS Engineer Corps, a company of sappers and miners from Memphis under Captain William D. Pickett, a small gang of Irish laborers, plus several Tennessee infantry regiments. The engineers relied upon the Irish laborers for the completion of skilled tasks, while about 1,500 local slaves performed the bulk of the heavy work.

In "progress of construction" by September 1861, Fort Pillow eventually consisted of nine different works, extending about half a mile along the riverbank. Traverses were thrown up between every set of three guns in the water batteries. According to Federal reports after the fort's capture, the bluffs were about 80ft high, and "very precipitous and rugged, furnishing an excellent location for defense. The works erected at the base of the bluff and on the bank, at some distance from the river, are very well and carefully built for about fifty guns. The country about the fort is exceedingly uneven and rough, and presents the most formidable obstacles ... There are deep ravines, steep ascents, wild gorges, sudden and unexpected declivities on every hand."

Regarding the armament at Fort Pillow, on December 1, 1861, Captain Lynch reported to General Polk, "We have in all fifty-eight 32-pounder guns; fifty-seven of them are mounted and ready for use; the remaining one is not mounted, for want of a suitable carriage." Most of the landward defences were finished by that time. A broken inner defensive line was added in March 1862 to enable a smaller garrison to defend the fort if necessary. Within the greater enclosed area, which contained three hills divided by a Y-shaped ravine system, slaves cleared some parts and left the rest wooded. Following the Federal occupation in June 1862, a Northern correspondent reported of the massive earthworks surrounding Fort Pillow: "These breastworks are far superior, considering their length, to any others

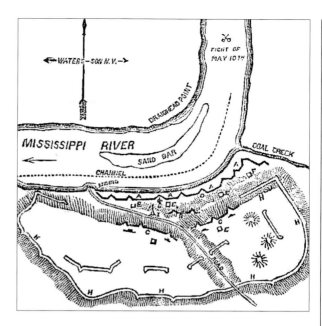

Printed in the New York *Herald* on June 12, 1862, this plan of Fort Pillow shows the extent of this large Confederate fortification. (A) indicates the water batteries lining the river shore; (B) represents a battery half way up the bluff; (C) shows the batteries on top of the bluff; (D) indicates a granite embrasure; (E) signifies magazines; (F) an unopened magazine; and (H) log and earthen breastworks. (Author's collection)

Based on an original sketch by Frank Vizetelly after the Confederate evacuation of Fort Pillow, Tennessee, this engraving was published in the *Illustrated London News* on July 12, 1862, and features the granite water battery carved from an outcrop on the First Chickasaw Bluffs. Removed from their carriages, the tubes for several spiked 32-pounder cannon are abandoned on the banquette tread. An empty revetted platform for a light gun is seen in the foreground. (Author's collection)

Another *Illustrated London News* engraving shows one of the abandoned water batteries at Fort Pillow with wooden gun carriages in the foreground and spiked 32-pounder cannon tubes strewn across the parapet. (Author's collection)

which I have seen during the war. Usually they were merely thrown up embankments of earth but these are regularly and scientifically made with broad parapets, heavy escarpments and counterscarps neatly lined with timber and firmly secured by deeply driven posts."

The Confederate evacuation of Fort Pillow on June 5, 1862 resulted from the fall of Island No.10 and the loss of Corinth after the battle of Shiloh. Federal naval forces under Flag Officer Charles H. Davis occupied the post the next day. With the neutralization of Fort Pillow and capture of New Orleans, the Union had a firm grip on the Mississippi River at both extremes of the Confederacy.

A force of approximately 1,500 Confederate troops under General Nathan Bedford Forrest stormed and captured a Union-built redoubt in Fort Pillow on April 12, 1864, killing many of the African American defenders. Often called the "Fort Pillow Massacre," it became one of the greatest atrocity stories of the Civil War. Charged with ruthless killing, Forrest argued that the black soldiers had been killed trying to escape. However, racial animosity on the part of his command was an undeniable factor.

Fort Wright (Randolph), 1861–62

Located in West Tennessee on the Mississippi River 65 miles above Memphis, the fortifications of Fort Wright were begun before the end of April 1861 under Captain Stockton, CS Army, when a gang of 27 slaves bound down river to Mississippi were loaned free of charge to the city authorities by a Kentucky plantation owner. Stockton was assisted by Major Lynch and Captain Champeny, with the works under the immediate charge of Captain Pickett and Lieutenant Wintters, of the Memphis Sappers and Miners. The Louisville *Weekly Journal* for June 11 of that year reported, "At Randolph there are 50 cannon, mostly thirty-two pounders; the rest larger, 42's and 64's. Thirty-two of them are mounted." Eleven days later a reporter for the Memphis *Bulletin* visited the fort and wrote:

There are some striking peculiarities about this stronghold. In ascending the hights [sic] which command the mighty river for ten or twelve miles, one is constantly surprised by encountering troops and heavy guns where these are least expected. The earthen breastworks have been sodded with grass, and on the exterior do not differ in appearance from other portions of the rugged hights [sic]. The visitor is constantly surprised by finding himself at the very cannon's mouth. The earthworks are from twenty to thirty feet in thickness, and are no less defensible on the river than on the landward side. In both directions nature has made the fortifications almost inaccessible … There is but one narrow defile on the landward side by which it is possible for an attacking force to reach the defenses: this is defended by heavy guns which sweep the defile for more than a mile. This pass is crossed by an earthen wall thirty or forty feet in thickness, and a quarter or a half mile east of this on the hill side, commanding the valley, is a crescent shaped wall [or lunette] with the open side next the main fortifications.

While Flag Officer Davis steamed down to occupy Fort Harris, the Union Ram fleet under Colonel Charles Ellet, Jr. weighed anchor at Fort Wright, which was also abandoned by the Confederates. Finding guns dismounted and hundreds of cotton bales used to strengthen the earthworks still smoldering, he demanded the surrender of the nearby town of Randolph, and hoisted the national flag over the fort.

Fort Harris, 1861–62

Established about six miles above Memphis near the mouth of the Loosahatchie River, on the Third Chickasaw Bluff, and named for Governor Isham Harris, Fort Harris was planned and constructed under the supervision of Captain Pickett, commanding the company of Sappers and Miners of Memphis, during April 1861. Visiting the site on April 29, a correspondent for the Memphis *Daily Appeal* reported:

> Through the politeness of the officers we were allowed to examine the profile of the work, and find that it is contemplated to inclose [sic] one hundred and fifty square feet, with an earthwork of sixty-four feet base and twenty-four feet between the perpendiculars, with an elevation of twenty-five feet above the river at an ordinary stage of water. It is calculated that the fort will furnish ample room for the garrisoning of one thousand men, for military stores to hold out for sixty days, and strength sufficient to repel a siege by ten thousand men for the same length of time. The guns will be stationed so as to have complete command of the river for a distance of two miles and a half – one mile and a half above, and one mile below the fortification – and be able to riddle anything in the shape of a river craft that sits upon the surface of the water within that distance. The labor upon the fortification has been progressing but a few days, and we were agreeably surprised to find it assuming shape and dimension in every way … There were two hundred and eighty laborers engaged on the work yesterday, and we understand that one hundred more were expected to be employed to-day. Much of the work has been done by gratuitous labor, the patriotic citizens of the surrounding country sending in their hands in large numbers – regarding it as a labor of love. One gentleman from Arkansas furnished one hundred hands, while another furnishes a number of hands and superintends a division of the labor in person.

On May 5, 1861 a request appeared in the Memphis *Daily Appeal* for 200 "negro men" to clear away the timber around Fort Harris. Work on Fort Harris progressed steadily and by June 11, 1861 the *Weekly Journal* of Louisville, Kentucky was able to report: "At Fort Harris there are four [guns] mounted, and ten or twelve ready to mount."

Memphis, 1861–64

The original Confederate fortifications at Memphis, begun in early June 1861, and including cotton-bale breastworks, were constructed by local slaves and free blacks under the supervision of a group of citizen volunteers, commanded by

Based on another Alex Simplot sketch, this 1862 engraving shows the levee at Memphis after the Federal occupation. Union troops are seen loading sugar cane and cotton onboard steamboats for transportation north. (Author's collection)

Captain William Pickett, who raised a company of sappers and miners among the "civil engineers, architects and mechanics" of the city. By June 7, the local press reported: "Breastworks have been built along the whole front of the bluff; some of the streets have already been barricaded; the fort at the mouth of Wolf river is rapidly progressing; a second fort will be raised below Titus' cotton shed. A redoubt opposite the Bradley block is far advanced toward completion." Another fort, or battery, was begun in front of the Exchange building on June 11. By September 15, 1861 a battery containing six 32-pounders, plus barbettes for two more guns, had been established on Jefferson Street, while the "Navy-yard Battery" consisted of two 32-pounders and two 64-pounders. By the end of the year, Fort Pickering had been established on the site of an original fort of the same name built on the South Bluffs in 1798. Earthworks in the Civil War fort included two ancient Indian mounds, which were converted into redoubts. The largest, known as the Chisca Mound, was a four-gun redoubt with an interior magazine, while the smaller mound, possibly called Jackson's Mound, became a three-gun redoubt.

The Union fleet of seven gunboats and rams under Flag Officer Davis and Colonel Ellet arrived off Memphis at 4.00 am on June 6, 1862. After a short one-and-a-half hour battle watched by the civilian population from the Chickasaw Bluffs, the small Confederate River Defense Fleet commanded by Captain James E. Montgomery was smashed, with all but one vessel sunk. Confederate survivors retreated down river towards Vicksburg, Mississippi, and Memphis, an important commercial and economic center on the Mississippi River, had fallen, opening another section of the Mississippi River to Union shipping.

Using newly recruited black troops, the Union army enlarged and expanded the works around Fort Pickering after the capture of Memphis. According to an 1864 report by Major General Q. A. Gillmore, Inspector General of Fortifications in the Military Division of West Mississippi, the gorge, or river front, was:

> one mile and a half in length, measured in a straight line between the extreme right and left flanks, while the depth of the work, measured at right angles to the river, at no point exceeds one-third of a mile, the

Established in 1846 but abandoned by 1854, the old US Navy Yard at Memphis included a pre-war battery that was strengthened to become one of the main Confederate water batteries defending the city in 1861. By September of that year it contained two 32-pounders and two 64-pounders. Based on a drawing by David Hunter Strother, alias "Porte Crayon," this engraving appeared in *Harper's Weekly* on March 15, 1862. (Author's collection)

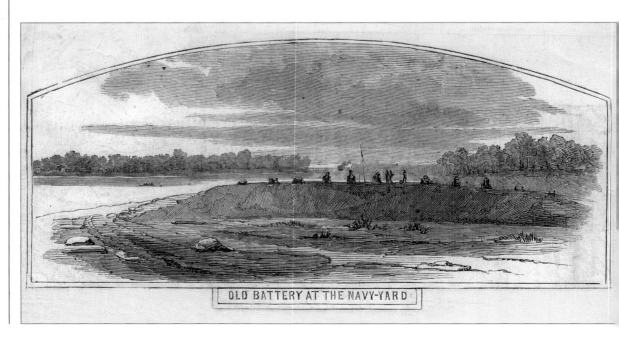

OLD BATTERY AT THE NAVY-YARD

20

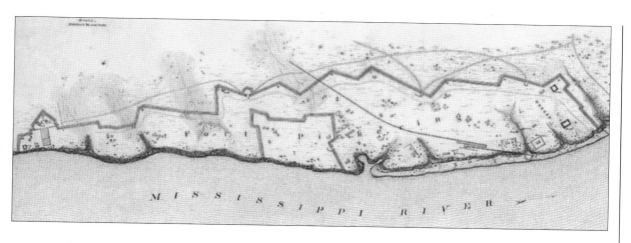

average depth being less than one-fourth of a mile ... The right and left of the line are extended down the river-bank to the water by a stockade. In advance of the ditch, and within buckshot range of the parapet, there is a row of inclined palisading [or fraise] which would be a formidable obstacle to an assaulting column.

The area enclosed in Fort Pickering contained supply houses, depots, horse corrals, and barracks with 12 lettered redans and batteries. Four outworks were planned but never built. Twelve numbered outer batteries circled the city to the east. Much of the earlier construction was performed by slave labor and free blacks, under the supervision of Captain Hoepner, of the engineer department.

Commanding the District of Memphis by July, 1862, Sherman reported progress at Fort Pickering to Grant on October 4:

The fixed batteries – 24-pounders, 32-pounders, and 8-inch howitzers – twenty-two in number, are mounted, four on the large [Chisca] mound, three on the small, five on the north battery, and remainder at the salients. I have four infantry companies detailed and instructed to handle these guns, and they have painted the guns and carriages, piled the shot and shell, and are now revetting with brick the breast-height. On the whole the fort is ready for battle. Much work yet remains to be done, but the lines are ready for defense.

I have embraced in the fort an immense cotton-shed, which furnishes fine storage to provisions, forage, camp and garrison equipage, and all things needful for a siege, and I have all my division staff in the lines. I occupy a house just across the street. A new magazine is substantially done. Two powder-houses under the bluff are full of ammunition, and I have converted an old brewery into an ordnance shop for the repair of arms, by which we can save all broken muskets, &c. Two good roads are finished to the water within the fort, so that steamboats can land our stores there. The brush to the south of the fort is cut down to the extent of a mile.

By 1864 Fort Pickering also contained a large keep constructed on an irregular quadrilateral open on the side next the river, with its flanks, like those of the main work, resting on the riverbank. The armament by this time had been increased to include "102 pieces of all calibers, viz: Forty-four 32-pounders, ten 8-inch sea-coast howitzers, four 8-inch columbiads, one 10-inch columbiad, four 24-pounder siege guns, six 8-inch siege howitzers, and thirty-three field pieces." Fort Pickering continued to serve as a major Union staging area throughout the Vicksburg campaign and until the end of the war.

Established in the southern part of Memphis by the Confederates, Fort Pickering was expanded by the Federals following the capture of the city on June 6, 1862. With earthworks containing 12 redans and batteries, it became a major supply base for Grant's army during the Vicksburg campaign. (Library of Congress)

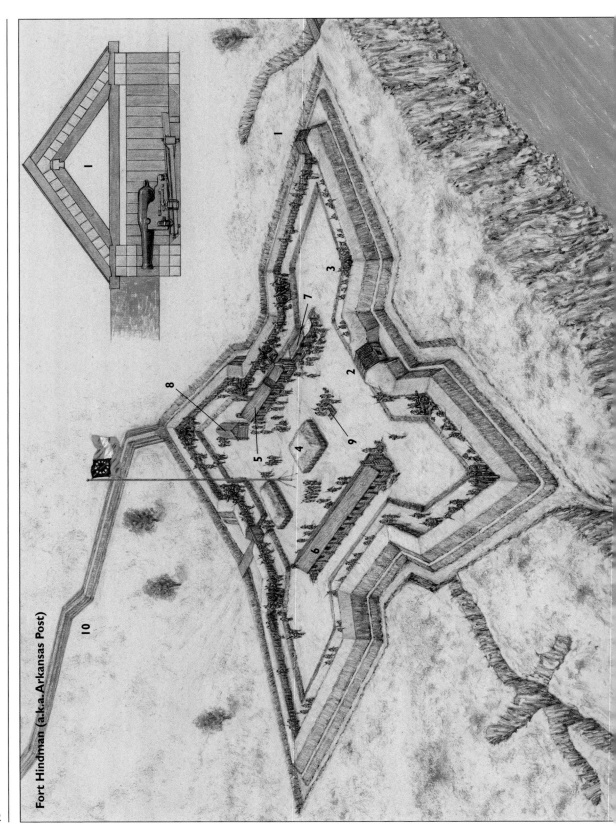

Fort Hindman (a.k.a. Arkansas Post)

Fort Hindman (a.k.a. Post of Arkansas), 1862–63

In October 1862 General John A. McClernand received President Lincoln's approval for an operation against Vicksburg. However, neither Halleck in Washington, DC, nor Grant, in whose department the operation would take place, were consulted. Instead of attacking Vicksburg, McClernand decided to capture Fort Hindman.

Established early in the summer of 1862 near the village of Arkansas Post, about 50 miles up the Arkansas River, at a point from which the Confederates were able to send gunboats into the Mississippi, Fort Hindman was a square, full-bastioned work on a bluff about 25ft above the water line, with a 4,500-strong garrison commanded by Brigadier General T. J. Churchill. Construction of the fort was entrusted to Colonel John W. Dunnington, who was assisted by CS engineer officers Captain Robert H. Fitzhugh and A. M. Williams. Clarkson's company of Sappers and Miners, plus a gang of slaves, provided the labor. In his battle report following its capture, McClernand described this fort as follows:

This hand-colored lithograph depicts the Federal bombardment and capture of Fort Hindman, also known as Arkansas Post, on January 11, 1863. (Library of Congress LC-USZC2-1987)

Fort Hindman (a.k.a. Arkansas Post)

Established near the village of Arkansas Post in the summer of 1862 at a point on the Arkansas River from which the Confederates were able to send gunboats into the Mississippi, Fort Hindman was a square, full-bastioned star fort on a bluff about 25ft above the water line. Its parapets were 18ft wide at the superior slope, or top, with a ditch 20ft wide and 8ft deep. The interior slope or inner face of the parapet was lined with a mixture of gabions and sod revetment. Three gun platforms were placed in each bastion and one in the curtain wall facing north. Each of these had a wooden plank platform. The casemate on the southern face of the northeastern bastion (**1**, also shown in cutaway form) was 18 × 15ft wide and 7½ft high, the walls being constructed of three thicknesses of oak timber 16in. square, with a pitched roof of the same dimensions with an additional revetment of iron bars or railroad track. This casemate contained a 9in. Columbiad. A similar casemate (**2**) – Casemate No. 2 – was constructed in the curtain facing the river, containing an 8in. Dahlgren gun.

Another 9in. Columbiad was mounted in the salient angle of the southeastern bastion on a barbette carriage (**3**). All three of these guns commanded the river below the fort. Beside these there were four 3in. Parrott guns and four 6-pounder iron smoothbore guns mounted on field carriages on the platforms in the fort. Inside the fort was a well-stored, earth-covered magazine with gabion revetment (**4**). The officers (**5**) and men's quarters (**6**), plus storehouse (**7**) and hospital (**8**) were wooden-frame buildings with pitched or lean-to shingle roofs. The well would have been covered to afford protection from heat (**9**). The entrance to the fort probably had wooden gates but was also protected by an earth and gabion traverse just inside the terreplein, or parade ground. A broken line of rifle-pits extended westerly from the salient angle of the northwestern bastion for 720 yards toward the bayou from its northwestern side (**10**). This was intersected by wooden gabion traverses. Four 6-pounder guns served by the Dallas Battery were mounted along these rifle-pits. Fort Hindman was garrisoned by 4,500 men commanded by Brigadier General T. J. Churchill.

The exterior sides of the fort, between the salient angles, were each 300 feet in length; the faces of the bastions two-sevenths of an exterior side and the perpendiculars one-eighth. The parapet was 18 feet wide on the top, the ditch 20 feet wide on the ground level, and 8 feet deep, with a slope of 4 feet base. A banquette for infantry was constructed around the interior slope of the parapet; also three platforms for artillery in each bastion and one in the curtain facing north. On the southern face of the northeastern bastion was a casemate 18 by 15 feet wide and 7½ feet high in the clear, the walls of which were constructed of three thicknesses of oak timber 16 inches square, and so the roof with an additional revetment of iron bars. One of the shorter sides of the casemate was inserted in the parapet and was pierced by an embrasure 3 feet 8 inches on the inside and 4 feet 6 inches on the outside, the entrance being in the opposite wall. This casemate contained a 9-inch columbiad. A similar casemate was constructed in the curtain facing the river, containing an 8-inch columbiad, and still another 9-inch columbiad was mounted in the salient angle of the southeastern bastion on a center-pintle barbette carriage. All of these guns commanded the river below the fort. Beside these there were four 3-inch Parrott guns and four 6-pounder iron smooth-bore guns mounted on field carriages on the platforms in the fort, which also contained a well-stored magazine, several frame buildings, and a well. The entrance to the fort, secured by a traverse, was on its northwestern side, and from the salient angle of the northwestern bastion extended a broken line of rifle-pits westerly for 720 yards toward the bayou, intersected by wooden traverses. Along the line of rifle-pits six field pieces were mounted, of which three were rifled.

Consisting of about 30,000 men in 50 transports escorted by 13 gunboats, McClernand's army hove to three miles below the fort during the night of January 9, 1863. A brigade with supporting cavalry and artillery, under General Peter Osterhaus, was landed on the west bank to prevent a Confederate retreat across the river. The remaining force landed on the east bank, and by 11.00 a.m., January 10 started to surround the fort from the land side. The Confederate pickets were driven in from the outlying earthworks, and the main assault involving a co-ordinated attack of land and naval forces finally began the next day. By 3.00 a.m., the defenders had been silenced and Admiral Porter entered the fort from USS *Black Hawk*, and was met by white flags. When informed of McClernand's action, Grant ordered him to withdraw immediately, as his force was needed for the forthcoming Vicksburg campaign. Fort Hindman was subsequently destroyed by order of General McClernand.

Fort Pemberton (a.k.a. Fort Greenwood), 1863
In an attempt to reach Vicksburg via the Yazoo Pass, Grant cut the Mississippi River levee in February 1863, which flooded the several bayous between the Mississippi and Tallahatchie rivers, making a navigable connection. Twenty-two transports carrying approximately 5,000 troops, two ironclads, two rams and six light draft gunboats made up the first expedition, which was later reinforced with another brigade and additional vessels. It took several weeks to make the 200-mile trip through the narrow and tortuous bayous.

Meanwhile, Confederate General John C. Pemberton ordered a fort to be constructed to block the enemy forces. Hastily erected near Greenwood, Mississippi near the junction of the Yazoo and Tallahatchie rivers 90 miles north of Vicksburg, Fort Pemberton barred the approach of the Union army via the Yazoo Pass. Named for General Pemberton, and described by its commander, Major General W. W. Loring, as a "line of works composed of cotton bales and earth," and by the Federals as being "situated on a knoll made inaccessible by a swamp and mounting heavy guns," it was erected under the supervision of Captain P. Robinson, of the CS Engineers, between February 24 and April 8, 1863.

Defended by a Confederate force of 5,000 men, the main part of this fort consisted of a sunken redan measuring 35ft in breadth and 8ft in depth, protected by earth-covered cotton bales two tiers high and six tiers deep. The embrasures were described as having a "one foot splay, revetted with sheet iron which blew out soon" when the fort came under fire.

On April 7, 1863 Colonel C. A. Fuller, Confederate Inspector-General of Heavy Artillery, reported that the armament of Fort Pemberton consisted of eight guns mounted en barbette as follows:

Commencing on the left, No. 1, banded 32-pounder rifle … manned by a detachment from the navy … No. 2, 8-inch shell (navy) gun, on naval carriage, manned by detachment from Twenty-first Louisiana Regiment. No. 3, 12-pounder rifle, on siege carriage, manned by a detachment from Waul's Legion … No. 4, 3-inch (18-pounder bolt) Whitworth gun, on field carriage, manned by detachment from Point Coupee (Louisiana) Battery … Nos. 5 and 6, two 12-pounder rifle guns, siege carriages … No. 7, 3-inch Parrott, and No. 8, 3.67-inch Parrott (Lady Richardson), in charge of Twenty-second Louisiana … Between Nos. 4 and 5 is a brass 6-pounder in battery, and on the left (exterior) of the fort are one 6-pounder and one 3-inch rifle, on field carriages.

As Federal forces approached, Loring cut the levees and flooded the surrounding area, ensuring that the only approach to the fort was by water. To further impede the enemy, the main channels of both rivers were blocked by sunken steamers. The Federal Flotilla arrived at Fort Pemberton on March 11, 1863, and the two ironclads attacked at 1,000 yards, but both were damaged after several attempts to reduce the fort. The entire Federal fleet eventually retired to the Mississippi River, and Grant failed to reach Vicksburg by the Tallahatachie/Yazoo route. During this battle General Loring won the sobriquet of "Old Blizzards" by standing on the cotton-bale parapet and shouting, "Give them blizzards, boys! Give them blizzards!"

Forts Cobun and Wade, 1863

About 40 miles below Vicksburg, Grand Gulf stood at the confluence of the Mississippi and Big Black rivers. Although the town was burned down by Federal forces on June 24, 1862, Confederates commanded by General John S. Bowen established powerful batteries at this location. Fortifications were begun in March 1863, and consisted of two large batteries. Fort Cobun, also known as the Upper Battery, was constructed on a limestone shelf overlooking the mouth of the Big Black River. Manned by Company A, 1st Louisiana Heavy Artillery, under Captain Henry Grayson, its armament consisted of one 30-pounder Parrott rifle, two 32-pounder rifled guns, and one 8in. naval gun, and contained a hot-shot furnace and two ammunition magazines. Also known as the Lower Battery, Fort Wade faced up the Mississippi towards the riverside township of Hard Times, and was manned by the 1st Missouri Light Artillery, commanded by Captain William Wade, and Guibor's Missouri Battery, under Captain Henry Guibor. These units served an 8in. shell gun and a 32-pounder rifle. A masked rifle trench containing about 100 sharpshooters ran along the top of the bluffs, while a "covered way" in the rear was large enough to shelter an entire regiment. Towards the end of March 1863, General Bowen, who had been a civil engineer before the war, requested permission to construct an ironclad revolving gun tower to supplement these defenses, but this was not begun in time to meet the Federal attack.

When Farragut's squadron passed Grand Gulf on March 31, 1863 the guns of Fort Wade roared into action. Bowen had a narrow escape when one of the 20-pounder Parrotts burst as he entered the emplacement. On April 29, four of Admiral David D. Porter's ironclads came down river past Vicksburg, and took up position a quarter of a mile from Fort Wade. A terrible artillery duel ensued

William Wing Loring

William Wing "Old Blizzards" Loring was born in 1818 in Wilmington, North Carolina, and was involved in soldiering from the age of 14 when he volunteered for service in the Seminole Wars in Florida. He served with distinction in the Mexican War and fought at Cerro Gordo, Contreras and Churubusco. At Mexico City, he led an assault on Belen Gate and lost an arm. Remaining in the US Army when the Mexican conflict ended, he commanded the Department of Oregon from 1849 to 1851, served on the frontier, fought Indians on the Rio Grande and on the Gila in Arizona. After participation in the Utah Expedition, he spent a year in Europe studying foreign armies before taking command of the Department of New Mexico from 1860 to 1861. At 38 years of age, he was the youngest line colonel of the US Army when the Civil War began. Entering Confederate service, he was promoted to brigadier general and served in Virginia. Following a dispute with Thomas J. Jackson he was promoted to major general and transferred to the West. When he led the successful Confederate defense of Fort Pemberton at Yazoo Pass in March 1863, he unwittingly earned the nickname "Old Blizzards." Personally directing fire, he cried in the heat of battle, "Give them blizzards, boys! Give them blizzards!"

and Fort Wade was enveloped by the storm of shot and shell delivered by the five gunboats. Two 32-pounder rifles were dismounted, and the parapet knocked to pieces. Captain Wade had his head blown off. By 11.00 a.m. Fort Wade had been silenced and Porter's entire squadron next concentrated its fire on Fort Cobun. The big guns at the latter post continued to roar out in defiance. Defeated in his efforts to overcome the Confederates in this larger fortification, Porter called off the attack. Under cover of darkness, the Federals by-passed Grand Gulf and crossed the Mississippi at Brainsburg the next morning, forcing the Confederate evacuation of Fort Cobun.

The up-river campaign

New Orleans, 1861–65

Although of immense commercial and strategic importance as the gateway to the Mississippi Valley, the port city of New Orleans did not become the focus of Northern operations until November 15, 1861, when Federal authorities approved a joint army–navy operation to capture it. The "Crescent City" was defended by a large force of militia under General Mansfield Lovell that was dispersed among a number of small earthworks guarding the many water approaches to the city. About 90 miles down river were two permanent masonry forts – Fort Jackson on the west bank and Fort St. Philip about 800 yards farther north on the east bank.[1]

In anticipation of a Federal assault down the Mississippi from Cairo, the city authorities appointed a military commission to plan and build a system of defenses to the north of New Orleans as early as July 1861. On July 15, Benjamin Suisson, President of the Commission, issued a "Notice to Woodchoppers" regarding the "Fortifications of New Orleans" requesting proposals within five days for the delivery "at different points situated a few miles above and below the city, on both sides of the river, [of] twelve thousand round logs of cypress or pine, with the bark on; said logs of 8 to 10 inches in diameter and 30 feet in length." Probably for use on banquette tread and slopes, he also asked for "proposals for furnishing two hundred thousand feet of pine timber and boards to order." On August 10, the City Council voted $100,000 to fund the building of defenses, which were placed under the supervision of Major Martin Luther Smith, of the CS Engineer Department.

Despite heavy rain the line of defenses above New Orleans, called "Victor Smith's Line" in compliment for the son of Major Smith, and later known as the "Parapet line," were well under way by mid-September. They were under the immediate charge of Lieutenant Benjamin Morgan Harrod, an engineer on the staff of Smith. A native of New Orleans, Harrod had at his disposal 325 workmen under the supervision of three local contractors. Intended to mount 14 guns between the bank and the swamp, the one-and-a-half-mile-long earthworks were unfinished when the city was captured. Also above the city, a line of fortifications

BELOW TOP This pre-Civil War lithograph showing a bird's-eye view of New Orleans was produced by J. Bachman and illustrates the importance of the city and its port. (Library of Congress: LC-USZC2-1987)

BELOW BOTTOM The earthworks constructed to defend up-river New Orleans were known as "Victor Smith's Line," or the "Parapet line," while those down river were called the "Chalmette line" on the right bank and the "McGehee line" on the left bank of the river. None of these fortifications were tested as the Federal fleet simply by-passed them after the capture of Forts Jackson and St. Philip near the mouths of the Mississippi and steamed into New Orleans. (Official Military Atlas of the Civil War)

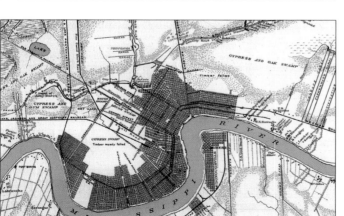

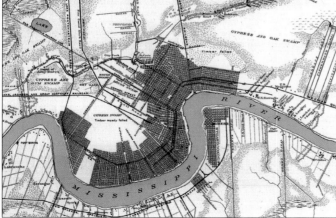

---

[1] See Fortress 6: *American Civil War Fortifications (1): Coastal Brick and Stone Forts.*

stretching from the river to the swamp, and known as the "Barataria line," ran along the south side of the Company's Canal.

Earthworks thrown up to protect the approaches between New Orleans and Lake Pontchartrain consisted of a two-gun battery in "a continuous line" across the Gentilly Ridge; another two-gun battery, together with supporting infantry works, guarding the Carrollton Railroad from Lake Pontchartrain; and further batteries commanding the Bayou St. John and Shell roads. Defenses below the city consisted of the "Chalmette line," built on the site of the British defeat on January 8, 1815, and stretching from the right bank of the river to the swamp, while the "McGehee line" served the same purpose on the opposite bank. Both of these works contained six-gun batteries.

Following the Federal occupation on December 3, 1861 of Ship Island, which guarded the approach to Lake Pontchartrain, the Confederate authorities in New Orleans began to prepare for the inevitable enemy assault. On February 27, 1862 the city militia was ordered into a camp of instruction outside the city but within "the lines of fortification." When the Federal fleet forced its way past Forts Jackson and St. Philip, and the batteries on the Chalmette and McGehee lines, on April 24–25, the remainder of the city fortifications were rendered useless and Farragut found them deserted when he continued up the river to capture the city. General Lovell had withdrawn 4,000 troops and turned the city over to the civil authorities, who surrendered New Orleans on April 29, 1862.

Following the Federal occupation, the "Parapet line," also known by then as the "Camp Parapet Fortifications," was rebuilt and renamed Fort John M. Morgan. A redoubt (including ten redans) was also added at this time.

Port Hudson, 1863

Situated on the east bank of the Mississippi about 25 miles north of Baton Rouge, Port Hudson was first occupied by Confederate forces under General John Breckinridge on August 15, 1862, and the construction of fortifications began almost immediately.

The site was an excellent natural location for building a fortress. The east bank of the river rose steeply in bluffs 80ft high, while the river bent sharply, making that stretch of the river even more of an obstacle for ships attempting to pass. Port Hudson was also an ideal place to defend from most landward

The Confederate water batteries at Port Hudson bombard Farragut's fleet during his passage up the river to Vicksburg on March 14–15, 1863. Sunk during this action, the USS *Mississippi* can be seen on fire at the rear of the column of vessels. (Author's collection)

directions, as bayous, thickets, and gullies protected the approaches. It also guarded the nearby mouth of the Red River, a route for goods flowing from the west that helped sustain the Confederacy.

By the spring of 1863 the Confederates, then commanded by Major General Franklin Gardner, had built massive parapets with about 30 siege guns mounted along the bluffs to command the river. According to an inspection report produced by Colonel Charles M. Fauntleroy, dated January 12, 1863: "The several batteries upon the bold river front, extending over a mile, are very formidable, both from their commanding position and number and character of the guns in position, except perhaps the two 32-pounders under the bluff called the Water Battery [between Batteries III and IV]." Fauntleroy was also critical of the location of the magazines which he considered "so immediately upon the bank and built so high above it as to render probable the destruction of each and all of them by the shells of the enemy." During the siege of Port Hudson two of these guns including a 10in. Columbiad nicknamed "Lady Davis" (known as the "Old Demoralizer" among Northern troops) were turned inland to fire over the other Confederate positions.

Also constructed was a line of earthen parapets, breastworks, and rifle pits along a perimeter of approximately 4½ miles surrounding the town of Port Hudson. Describing these defenses from south to north, an officer of the Confederate garrison recorded: "For about three-quarters of a mile from the river the line crossed a broken series of ridges, plateaus and ravines, taking advantage of high ground in some places and in others extending down a steep declivity; for the next mile and a quarter it traversed Gibbon's and Slaughter's fields where a wide level plain seemed formed on purpose for a battlefield; another quarter of a mile carried it through deep and irregular gullies, and for three-quarters of a mile more it led through fields and over hills to a deep gorge, in the bosom of which lay Sandy creek."

According to Colonel Fauntleroy, these field works consisted of "a crémaillere line, connected by redans and curtains, extending over the distance of 2½ miles, the most important portion of which has already been completed, whilst the remaining part is being pushed forward by a large addition recently to the negro force employed on the work." With these lines unfinished by January 1863, Fauntleroy concluded: "The general commanding at Port Hudson considers the most important portion of the entire defenses completed when he shall have connected the unfinished half mile of the work on the north side by a succession of rifle pits, nature having already assisted in the defense thereabout by a number of impracticable gorges."

By July 1863 these defenses consisted of some formidable field works, including a semi-detached redan at the northeast corner, dubbed "Fort Desperate" by Confederate troops to reflect the dire and hopeless situation in which the defenders found themselves. Below this in the eastern-facing lines was another redan called the "Priest's Cap," while "The Citadel," a high, well-fortified bluff, stood at the extreme southern end of the line, accompanied by advanced rifle pits known as the "Devil's Elbow."

The first action took place at Port Hudson on March 14, 1863 when Admiral Farragut bombarded its defenses during his passage up the river to Vicksburg. The USS *Mississippi* was sunk in this action. During the period May 8–10, Federal gunboats again bombarded it, and silenced the Confederate batteries. Union land forces, composed of the 19th Corps commanded by General Nathaniel Banks, next attacked Port Hudson and had their first engagement on May 26 on the Bayou Sara Road, four miles north of the city. The Confederate field works were unsuccessfully assaulted on May 27, June 11 and 14, following which a siege was conducted from May 27 through July 9, 1863, when Port Hudson finally surrendered. The siege cost the Union 3,000 men. Confederate losses were over 7,200, including 5,500 prisoners, two steamers, 60 guns, 5,000 small arms, 150,000 rounds of small-arms ammunition, and almost 45,000 pounds of gunpowder.

The fortifications of Vicksburg, 1862–63

In May 1863, President Abraham Lincoln had declared, "Vicksburg is the key! The war can never be brought to a close until that key is in our pocket." From mid-October 1862, Major General Ulysses S. Grant made several unsuccessful attempts to capture this river city, but Union efforts at Chickasaw Bluffs, and the Yazoo Pass and Steele's Bayou expeditions, came to nought. Thus, in the spring of 1863 Grant prepared to cross his troops from the west bank of the Mississippi River to a point south of Vicksburg, from where he would drive against the city from the south and east.

Confederate interest in the defense of Vicksburg began much earlier than these events. In response to the Federal occupation of Ship Island, in the Gulf of Mexico, on March 21, 1862, Colonel James L. Autry of the 27th Mississippi Infantry was ordered to the city as "Military Governor and Post Commandant," and began the first stages of fortification by the end of that month. Further reinforcements arrived at Vicksburg following the fall of New Orleans on April 25. Brigadier General Martin Luther Smith assumed command of Vicksburg on May 12, 1862 and the defense of the city became the overall responsibility of Lieutenant General John C. Pemberton on October 14, 1862. Some of the first works erected consisted of extensive fortifications and batteries on the bluffs above the Yazoo River about 12 miles upstream from Vicksburg at Snyder's ('Haynes') Bluff. Containing nine large guns and garrisoned by the 22nd Louisiana and 3rd Mississippi, totaling 1,300 men initially under the command of Colonel Edward Higgins, these works extended approximately two miles southward, blocking Union gunboats from raiding the fertile Yazoo River valley, and serving as an outpost of the main Vicksburg fortifications.

The "Great River Battery" was constructed by 1,400 black troops under the supervision of Major J. Bailey, 4th Wisconsin, acting engineer officer on the staff of General Sherman, in seven days during the siege of Port Hudson in June 1863. Protecting a combination of siege guns and lighter Napoleon cannon mounted behind embrasures, the parapet of this battery consisted of cotton bales and sandbags covered with earth. Note two men emerging from a bombproof in the right foreground. The Confederate fortifications across the Mississippi River consist of the "Citadel," which was described as "the highest and strongest work in Port Hudson." (Author's collection)

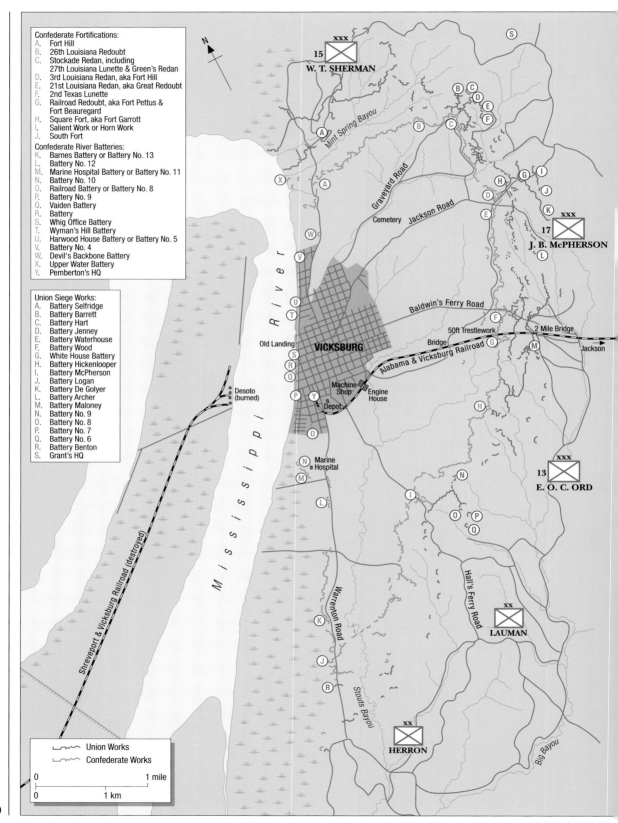

Confederate Fortifications:
A. Fort Hill
B. 26th Louisiana Redoubt
C. Stockade Redan, including
   27th Louisiana Lunette & Green's Redan
D. 3rd Louisiana Redan, aka Fort Hill
E. 21st Louisiana Redan, aka Great Redoubt
F. 2nd Texas Lunette
G. Railroad Redoubt, aka Fort Pettus &
   Fort Beauregard
H. Square Fort, aka Fort Garrott
I. Salient Work or Horn Work
J. South Fort

Confederate River Batteries:
K. Barnes Battery or Battery No. 13
L. Battery No. 12
M. Marine Hospital Battery or Battery No. 11
N. Battery No. 10
O. Railroad Battery or Battery No. 8
P. Battery No. 9
Q. Vaiden Battery
R. Battery
S. Whig Office Battery
T. Wyman's Hill Battery
U. Harwood House Battery or Battery No. 5
V. Battery No. 4
W. Devil's Backbone Battery
X. Upper Water Battery
Y. Pemberton's HQ

Union Siege Works:
A. Battery Selfridge
B. Battery Barrett
C. Battery Hart
D. Battery Jenney
E. Battery Waterhouse
F. Battery Wood
G. White House Battery
H. Battery Hickenlooper
I. Battery McPherson
J. Battery Logan
K. Battery De Golyer
L. Battery Archer
M. Battery Maloney
N. Battery No. 9
O. Battery No. 8
P. Battery No. 7
Q. Battery No. 6
R. Battery Benton
S. Grant's HQ

N

15 W. T. SHERMAN

17 J. B. McPHERSON

13 E. O. C. ORD

LAUMAN

HERRON

Mississippi River

VICKSBURG

Mint Spring Bayou

Graveyard Road

Cemetery

Jackson Road

Baldwin's Ferry Road

50ft Trestlework

Bridge

2 Mile Bridge

Jackson

Alabama & Vicksburg Railroad

Old Landing

Desoto (burned)

Machine Shop

Engine House

Depot

Marine Hospital

Warrenton Road

Hall's Ferry Road

Stouts Bayou

Big Bayou

Shreveport & Vicksburg Railroad (destroyed)

Union Works
Confederate Works

0 — 1 mile
0 — 1 km

30

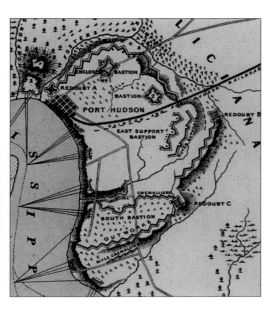

Construction of the main fortifications at Vicksburg was initially entrusted to Captain David B. Harris, Provisional Engineer Corps, CS Army, who was assisted by Acting Captain John M. Reid, and his son Acting Lieutenant John H. Reid, the labor being mostly completed by a force of about 3,000 slaves impressed from plantations in the adjacent counties. Major Samuel H. Lockett, CS Engineers, took over responsibility as Chief Engineer for the construction of the main Vicksburg fortifications on June 20, 1862. On November 1, Lockett was made Chief Engineer of the Department of Mississippi and East Louisiana, with responsibility for operations from Holly Springs, Mississippi, to Port Hudson, Louisiana, but never relinquished immediate charge of the defenses of Vicksburg. According to Lockett:

> At the time of my arrival no enemy was near, but the work of preparation was going on vigorously. The garrison was engaged in strengthening the batteries already constructed, in making bomb-proof magazines, and in mounting new guns recently arrived. Several new batteries were laid out by myself on the most commanding points above the city; these were afterward known as the "Upper Batteries." The work of making an accurate map of Vicksburg and vicinity was also begun.

The river defenses at Vicksburg, commanded by Colonel E. Higgins, consisted of 37 large-caliber guns, plus 13 field artillery pieces, distributed in 13 batteries covering three miles of waterfront. The most important works were the Water Battery, Wyman's Hill Battery, and the Marine Hospital Battery, all three of which stood 30–40ft above river level, which gave them the advantage of plunging fire, without the drawbacks of depressing the gun muzzles too far. (The projectiles of muzzle-loading artillery pieces had a tendency to "start," or shift forward, when the muzzle was depressed, with adverse effects on ballistics.) The most important of these batteries was the Water Battery. Manned by the 1st Tennessee Artillery, under Colonel Andrew Jackson, Jr., it commanded the sharp bend in the river. In April 1863, this battery mounted three 32-pounder rifles, one 32-pounder smoothbore, and one 10in. Columbiad. Wyman's Hill Battery, located on the northern outskirts of Vicksburg, and commanded by Major F. N. Ogden, 8th Louisiana Artillery Battalion, held three 10in. Columbiads, one 8in. Columbiad, one 32-pounder rifle, one 2.71in. Whitworth rifle, and one 3in. Armstrong rifle. Marine Hospital Battery, located south of Vicksburg, and manned by the

ABOVE LEFT This very fanciful map of Confederate defenses around Port Hudson, Louisiana, by Charles Sholl at least shows the extent of the earthworks around the city, although the inner bastions and many other features shown appear not to have existed. The fields of fire of the water batteries are an accurate illustration of the strength of firepower at this location. (National Park Service)

ABOVE RIGHT This interior view of the "Citadel," at the remote southern end of the Confederate defenses at Port Hudson, shows the "rat holes," or dug-out caves, burrowed into the base of their parapet to escape Union shells. (National Archives)

OPPOSITE PAGE The Vicksburg fortifications and siege lines.

31

Samuel H. Lockett

Samuel H. Lockett was born in Mecklenburg County, Virginia, on July 7, 1837. The son of Napoleon Lockett and Mary Clay Lockett, he grew up in Marion, Alabama, where he attended Howard College. In 1859 he graduated second in his class from the US Military Academy at West Point and was appointed to the Corps of Topographical Engineers. Resigning from his post in 1861, he accepted a commission in the Confederate army and, on June 20, 1862 was ordered to report to General Martin L. Smith as an engineer officer. He remained in that capacity until November 1 when he was appointed Chief Engineer of the Department of Mississippi and East Louisiana, with responsibility for operations from Holly Springs, Mississippi to Port Hudson, Louisiana. Retaining immediate charge of the defenses of Vicksburg, he carefully selected the best ground for its defense. The earthworks he supervised construction of between June 1862 and May 1863 "wrung every possible tactical advantage out of the dizzying landscape" surrounding Vicksburg, according to historians William L. Shea and Terrence J. Winschel. In his contribution to the monumental collection of essays in *Battles & Leaders* entitled "The Defense of Vicksburg," Lockett stated: "The most prominent points I purposed to occupy with a system of redoubts, redans, lunettes, and small field-works, connecting them by rifle-pits so as to give a continuous line of defense." As a result of his great skill as a military engineer, the Confederate forces under General Pemberton were able to hold off two full-scale Union assaults and withstood a 47-day siege. Following the surrender of Vicksburg, Lockett continued to serve as Chief Engineer on the staff of General D. H. Maury and supervised construction of the Mobile defenses. After the war he taught mathematics at the Louisiana State University, worked on the Louisiana Topographical Survey, and served as engineer for the Khedive of Egypt during the Abyssinian Campaign of 1875–76. He invented a surveying instrument called the odograph, and assisted Charles Stone draft plans for the pedestal for the Statue of Liberty. Assigned to Chile in 1888 to work on a large railroad and construction project, he died in Bogota, Colombia on October 12, 1891. His portrait was painted by Nicola Marschall, who briefly served as one of his draftsmen in Company B, 2nd Regiment, Confederate Engineer Troops. Marschall is believed to have designed the uniform for the Confederate Regular Army. (Alabama Department of Archives and History, Montgomery, Alabama)

1st Louisiana Artillery, under Lieutenant Colonel D. Beltzhoover, contained three 42-pounder smoothbores, two 32-pounder smoothbores, and two 32-pounder rifles. An abatis was constructed from the bluffs to the river at the southern end of the city water front to prevent the Federals from advancing across the flat marshland.

Following the unsuccessful Federal naval bombardment of Vicksburg between June 27 and July 25, 1862, Major Lockett repaired and strengthened the river batteries and, on September 1, began construction of a line of defense in the rear of Vicksburg. The engineer officer recalled:

A month was spent in reconnoitering, surveying, and studying the complicated and irregular site to be fortified. No greater topographical puzzle was ever presented to an engineer. The difficulty of the situation was greatly enhanced by the fact that a large part of the hills and hollows had never been cleared of their virgin forest of magnificent magnolia-trees and dense undergrowth of cane. At first it seemed impossible to find anything like a general line of commanding ground surrounding the city; but careful study gradually worked out the problem.

Much of the work on the Vicksburg defenses from December 1862 through April 1863 was under the direct supervision of Captain W. D. Pickett, commanding the Sappers and Miners, Tennessee Volunteers. During December 1862 this unit was engaged in laying out and superintending the building of the fortifications, and "mounting and dismounting guns on the river line, laying platforms and building magazines." A strong line of works was thrown up along the crest of a ridge that was fronted by a deep ravine plus a ditch 15ft wide and 10ft deep. The defense line began at the river's edge two miles above Vicksburg and curved for nine miles along the ridge to the river below, thus enclosing the city within an irregular shape representing a figure "7."

Artillery positions and forts, consisting of redans, lunettes, and redoubts, were constructed at salient and commanding points along the line. The earther walls of the forts were up to 25ft thick, with deep ditches in front. Between the strongpoints, which were located every few hundred yards along the line was constructed a line of rifle pits and entrenchments. Where spurs of land jutted out from the main ridge, advanced batteries were placed to provide a deadly crossfire against attacking forces. The Confederates mounted a total of 102 guns scattered among 77 positions sited to enfilade approaches to the city defenses.

Nine of the larger forts were constructed to command the six road approaches, plus one rail route, into Vicksburg. These roads followed ridges and high ground and were flanked on both sides by deep ravines and gullies. A series of redans, later called Fort Hill, stood near the river north of the city. The Twenty-sixth Louisiana Redoubt was established on the northern line of defenses about one mile from the riverbank. The Stockade Redan guarded the Graveyard Road, while the Third Louisiana Redan and the Twenty-first Louisiana Redan, or Great Redoubt, blocked the Jackson Road route. The Second Texas Lunette controlled the Baldwin's Ferry Road, and the Railroad Redoubt, also known as Fort Pettus, controlled the tracks of the Alabama and Vicksburg Railroad. Fort Garrott, also called the Square Fort, commanded the southeast approaches, while the Salient Works guarded the Hall's Ferry Road. South Fort stood at the southernmost point, on the river below Vicksburg. In constructing these fortifications, the Confederates left the rear of all the forts (bar the Square Fort) open, to give the garrisons an opportunity to counterattack, in the event of being driven out. When interviewed in 1894, Francis A. Shoup, who commanded a brigade of Louisiana troops in the Vicksburg defenses, including those in the Twenty-sixth Louisiana Redoubt, recalled: "The fortifications about Vicksburg were a poorly run and poorly constructed set of earthworks, but there was no point of the whole line which could not have been carried by a simple assault without ladders or any sort of machines." A series of rifle pits formed a ragged outer line of defense. Hastily dug and manned as Grant's army approached Vicksburg on May 18, 1863, these were abandoned as the Confederate pickets withdrew to their inner defenses.

The line from the river front north of the city to the Graveyard Road was placed under the command of General M. L. Smith; General John H. Forney commanded the line between the Graveyard Road and the railroad; and General Carter L. Stevenson occupied the line from the railroad to the South Fort near the river below the city. Captain D. Wintter, commanding the small company of sappers and miners, was assigned to the line commanded by generals Smith and Forney, while Captain Powhatan Robinson, CS Engineers, had direct responsibility for the line commanded by General Stevenson. Work on the defenses was generally performed by fatigue parties detailed from each command to work within the limits of its own lines.

Greatly strengthening the Confederate defenses was the irregular topography resultant from the peculiar characteristics of the loess soil of the region, which over the centuries had been cut into deep gullies and ravines by the action of running water. This resulted in a very broken terrain, which would seriously obstruct the operations of the Union army during its siege operations. To permit a clear field of fire and to further hinder the advancing enemy, all the trees in front of the Confederate line were cut down and formed into an abatis.

Taken inside a U-shaped redoubt called "Fort Desperate" in the northeast part of the Confederate fortifications after the surrender of Port Hudson on July 9, 1863, this photograph shows damaged 12-pounder cannon. In the background can be seen the interior of the reinforced parapet and the shallow trench just inside it, which provided additional shelter for the defenders. Also visible at rear left is a barrel with a hole cut through it, which was used as a shield by sharpshooters, who shot through the hole at the Union troops digging the sap towards the fort. Note how the ground slopes down sharply just outside the parapet. (National Archives)

At the start of the siege, which began on May 22, 1863, the Confederate Army of Vicksburg numbered about 31,000 men, of which General Pemberton listed 18,500 effectives as available to man his defenses. Most Confederate units remained at their posts in the trenches without relief throughout the entire siege. Grant gave his strength, shortly after the siege began, as about 50,000 effectives, and his army was steadily enlarged during the siege operations by reinforcement from Memphis.

The Confederate fortifications

Fort Hill

The series of redans including what was known to the citizens of Vicksburg as Fort Hill stood at the northern end of the Confederate lines. Running along Mint Spring Bluff, they anchored the Vicksburg defenses above the city to the Mississippi River. The main work served as an observation for the Water Battery below, and contained one 3in. rifle manned by Captain C. S. Johnston's Company, Tennessee Heavy Artillery, which was in position from May 19 until the end of the siege. This gun helped the river batteries sink the Federal gunboat *Cincinnati* on May 27, 1863. The rest of the line was garrisoned by elements of the brigade commanded by General John C. Vaughn, which consisted of the 60th, 61st, and 62nd Tennessee Infantry, and contained two 6-pounder guns and one 24-pounder siege gun in several small redans. Never directly assaulted during the siege, these earthworks were destroyed and built over with new defenses following the Union army's occupation of Vicksburg on July 4, 1863.

Twenty-Sixth Louisiana Redoubt

Established on a high ridge in the northern line of defenses about one mile from the river bank, the Twenty-Sixth Louisiana Redoubt consisted of a 6ft-high parapet with a total width of 20ft. The exterior ditch, which also served as a trench, was 10ft wide and 6ft deep. In front of this was a rough palisade and glacis. Behind the parapet was a 2ft-high firestep and a 20ft-wide terreplein. Beyond this was a 6ft-high and 12ft-wide traverse, which enclosed the parapet at its western end while leaving the eastern end open. The brigade, under General Francis A. Shoup, consisting of the 26th, 27th, and 28th Louisiana, garrisoned this redoubt and manned the trenches at its front and either side.

The Stockade Redan complex during the siege of Vicksburg
The Stockade Redan was the most northerly point in the defenses of Vicksburg. See the main text for full details.

1 The Central Redan (plus section view)
2 Green's Redan (plus section view)
3 Twenty-seventh Louisiana Lunette (plus section view)
4 The Graveyard Road
5 Palisade (plus section view)
6 Abatis

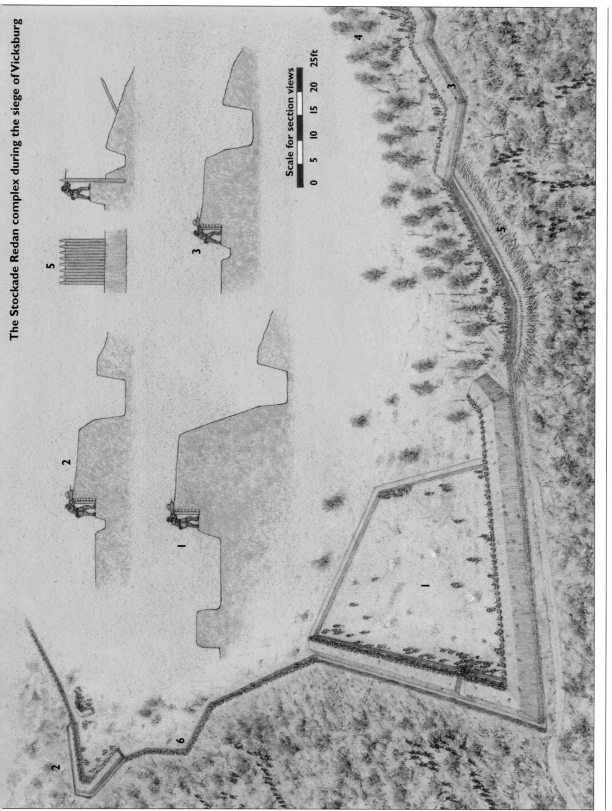

The Stockade Redan complex during the siege of Vicksburg

Scale for section views

0 5 10 15 20 25ft

This rare view behind the Confederate lines near the Stockade Redan at Vicksburg is based on a sketch made with "a glass" from the Federal rifle pits. The poplar-wood palisade is seen at center, while at left Confederate troops dig a rifle trench, which is possibly the beginning of the traverse behind the main redan. (Author's collection)

The Stockade Redan

The Stockade Redan was the principal work guarding the Graveyard Road approach to Vicksburg, and represented the northernmost point in the city defenses. The entire complex had a large redan at its center, linked at 75 yards to its right by rifle trenches to a smaller work called Green's Redan, and connected 150 yards to its left by a stockade to the Twenty-seventh Louisiana Lunette. Both the latter works provided enfilade fire over the ground in front of the central redan. This section of the defenses was garrisoned by elements of the brigades commanded by Colonel Francis M. Cockrell, General Martin E. Green (following his death, Colonel Thomas P. Dockery) under the division of Major General John S. Bowen, and General Louis Hébert's brigade from Major General John H. Forney's division.

On a prominence about 370ft above sea level, the face of the westerly salient of the central redan was slightly longer than its east face, and had an oblique angle at its extreme left end. Its rear was screened from enfilading fire by an angular-shaped, 8ft-high traverse which began at its easterly end and bisected its west face. The earthen parapets of the central redan were about 16ft wide and had a 17ft-high exterior slope beneath which was a 6ft-deep ditch. For much of the siege it contained one 12-pounder howitzer served by a section of the Appeal Battery, of Arkansas, which sat behind an embrasure in the eastern face, and was held by the 36th Mississippi and the 1st and 4th Missouri Consolidated.

Known later in the siege as Green's Redan, the smaller work to the right had 20ft-wide earthen parapets with 4½ft-high exterior slopes and 6ft-deep ditches behind which were 2ft-deep trenches. A six-pounder gun of Lowe's Missouri Battery, under Lieutenant Thomas B. Catron, stood behind a low parapet to the right and rear, with the 5th Missouri Infantry in support. It was in this work that Brigadier General Martin E. Green declared, "a bullet has not yet been molded that will kill me," just moments before he passed in front of an artillery embrasure and was slain by a Union sharpshooter. After June 2, 1863 Green's Redan was held by elements of the 20th Arkansas Infantry.

The parapets in the Twenty-seventh Louisiana Lunette to the left were of the same dimensions as Green's Redan, and contained a single 12-pounder gun of McNally's Arkansas Battery, commanded by Captain Joseph T. Hatch, in a small redan at its center, while the earthwork was defended by the 27th Louisiana Infantry, with the 2nd Missouri in support. To block the Graveyard Road and defend a ravine running between this lunette and the central redan, the connecting line, manned at times by the 3rd Missouri, was defended by a 9ft-high palisade of poplar logs between 9 and 12 inches in diameter. In front of this sat a 4ft-deep ditch, a glacis and abatis, plus dense natural vegetation. This lunette, part of the palisade to its right, and the line to its left, repulsed the Federal attacks on May 19 and 22, 1863. The Federal failure to overrun the fortifications at the Stockade Redan was a major factor in Grant's decision to avoid any more direct assaults on the Vicksburg defenses and to begin siege operations.

Third Louisiana Redan (Fort Hill)

Situated on a narrow ridge at the highest point in the area, about 380ft above sea level, and built to command the Jackson Road into Vicksburg, the Third Louisiana Redan, known to the Federals as Fort Hill, was garrisoned by the 3rd Louisiana, under Major David Pierson. It consisted of northern and southern salient angles with an eastern face containing a 20-pounder Parrott and a 3in. rifle piece manned by the Appeal Battery, commanded by Lieutenant Christopher C. Scott. Further earthworks, including a smaller redan either side, linked to rifle trenches manned by troops of Hébert's brigade, with the 43rd Mississippi at left and the 38th Mississippi at right. The earthen parapets in this work were about 24ft wide with a 10ft-high exterior slope running into a natural glacis formed by the edge of the ridge. This work also lacked an exterior ditch due to its precipitous position on the ridge.

These *Harper's Weekly* engravings show the miners at work deep under the Third Louisiana Redan (above), and a Confederate grenade exploding near the entrance to the Federal mine shaft (below). The tunnel, or half gallery, was 3ft wide, 4ft high, and 40ft long. (Author's collection)

Under the supervision of Captain A. Hickenlooper, Federal miners began mining operations under the Third Louisiana Redan, a.k.a. Fort Hill, on June 23, 1863, and two days later, at 3.30 p.m., 2,200 lb. of gunpowder was exploded in four different branches of the same mine, following which Hickenlooper was able to report, "Perfect success. Troops rushed in and took possession of crater, and detail of pioneer troops went to work under my direction clearing away entrance to same." Based on a sketch by Theodore Davis, this *Harper's Weekly* engraving shows the moment of explosion. (Author's collection)

In their efforts to break through the Confederate defenses, Federal forces advanced along the Jackson Road towards the Third Louisiana Redan on June 7, 1863 "under the cover of cotton bales placed on a [railroad] car," but were driven back when the defenders set the cotton on fire by firing musket balls wrapped in "turpentine and tow." The Federals also detonated two mines under the Third Louisiana Redan. The first, on June 25, created a crater 40ft wide and 12ft deep, where the point of the redan had once stood. Brigadier General Mortimer D. Leggett's brigade of Logan's division sent a regiment charging into the crater, supported by every gun within firing range. But the defenders of the redan had detected the mining operation and evacuated the work before this mine exploded, withdrawing to a 6ft-high parapet thrown up about 15ft behind the original earthworks. Fighting continued into the night in and around the crater, but when Cockrell's brigade, of Bowen's division, arrived to reinforce the Confederate line, any chance of a Union breakthrough vanished. This engagement cost the Federals 34 killed and 209 wounded. Confederate losses were 21 killed and 73 wounded. Among the former was Colonel Eugene Erwin, commander of the 6th Missouri Infantry and grandson of Henry Clay, who jumped up on the parapet at the height of the counterattack calling to his men, "Come on my brave boys, don't let the Third Regiment get ahead of you!"

The Federals immediately started another mine under the remnants of the redan. Detonated on July 1, this completed the destruction of this earthwork, but with consolidated Confederate lines in the rear of the redan, a Union assault was not forthcoming. A third mine was set for explosion as part of the planned attack for July 6, 1863.

The Battle in the Crater, showing the mine explosion beneath the 3rd Louisiana Redan

Towards the northern end of the Confederate defenses at Vicksburg, the Third Louisiana Redan was one of the major points of attack. After approaching with a sap called Logan's Approach, the Federals detonated the first of two mines on June 25, 1863. This created a crater 40ft wide and 12ft deep where the point of the redan had once stood. Brigadier General Mortimer D. Leggett's brigade of Logan's Federal division sent a regiment charging into the crater, supported by every gun within firing range.

However, the defenders of the redan, under Major David Pierson, had detected the mining operation and evacuated the work before this mine exploded, withdrawing to a 6ft-high parapet thrown up about 15ft behind the original earthworks. Fighting continued into the night in and around the crater, but when Cockrell's brigade, of Bowen's division, arrived to reinforce the Confederate line, any chance of a Union breakthrough vanished. This engagement cost the Federals 34 killed and 209 wounded. Confederate losses were 21 killed and 73 wounded.

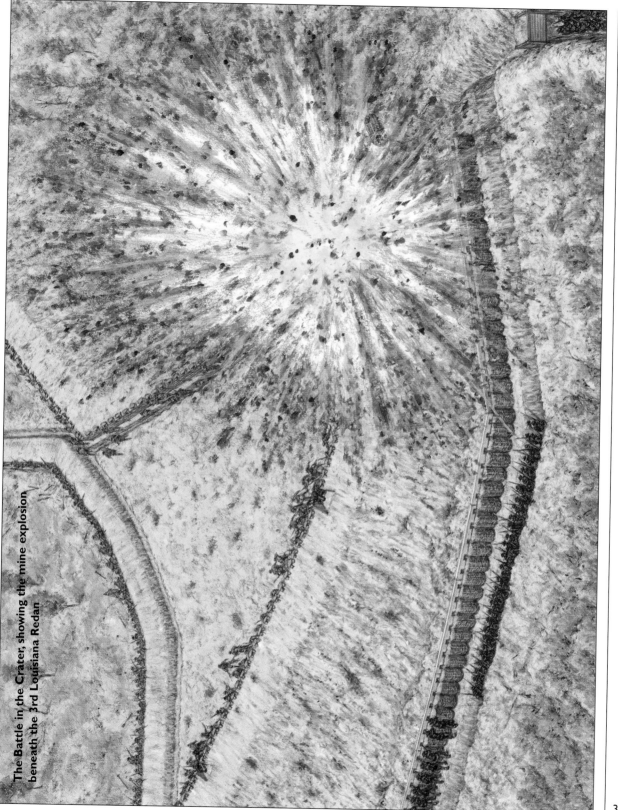

The Battle in the Crater, showing the mine explosion beneath the 3rd Louisiana Redan

The Federal mine that exploded under the Third Louisiana Redan on June 25, 1863 created a 40ft-wide crater and was the signal for attack. Detecting the imminent danger, the Confederate garrison withdrew to a hastily prepared parapet behind the main work and repelled the main assault after some of the most terrible hand-to-hand fighting of the Civil War. (Author's collection)

Twenty-first Louisiana Redan (Great Redoubt)

The Twenty-first Louisiana Redan was the largest Confederate fortification in the Vicksburg lines. Also known to the Federals as "the Great Redoubt," this strongpoint on a commanding ridge to the right of the Jackson Road consisted of four lunettes linked together by a 13ft-high parapet with a 16ft-wide by 8ft-deep ditch. Manned by the 21st Louisiana Infantry, Hébert's brigade, towards its center was a large lunette behind which was a curtain wall. Linked at its right by a parapet with parallel curtain wall was an irregular lunette. At the extreme left end of the parapet, and also overlooking the Jackson Road approach to Vicksburg, was an irregular lunette containing a single 12-pounder howitzer manned by the Appeal Battery. Immediately to the right of this was another small lunette containing two 3in. rifles served by the Pointe Coupee (Louisiana) Artillery, Co. B, commanded by Captain William A. Davidson. Both of these smaller lunettes had parapets only 4½ft high, with 2ft-deep ditches in the rear, which enabled the defenders to stand upright without direct exposure to enemy fire. During the assault on May 22, 1863 they unleashed a hail of lead on the Federal soldiers as they approached the formidable earthworks.

Second Texas Lunette

The Second Texas Lunette guarded the Baldwin's Ferry Road into Vicksburg, and was part of a complex, including the Railroad Redoubt and the Square Fort to the south, plus a smaller lunette about 100 yards behind and on the other side of the road, which provided enfilading fire from all directions. If it was to be successful, an assault on any one of these forts had to carry the others as well. The Second Texas Lunette was described thoroughly in a report by Colonel Ashbel Smith, 2nd Texas Infantry, dated July 10, 1863:

> Our fort was an irregular lunette, with no flank [or rifle pits] on the left; or it may be considered a redan with a large pan coupé, having its left thrown forward and its right retired. Its left having no flank, its interior was exposed to an enfilading and reverse fire from the enemy approaching by the valley, which debouches on its left. Its parapet was about 4¼ feet high on the inside, its superior slope about 14 feet thick. It was surrounded by a ditch in front nearly 6 feet deep, with an irregular glacis made by the natural slope of the earth to the ferry road. There were two embrasures for cannon, with a traverse between them … The men of my regiment were stationed as follows: the

two right companies occupied the rifle-pits tending off from the right of the fort; the four next companies manned the fort; the four remaining, or left, companies occupied the lines next on our left separated from the fort by the interval of upward of 100 yards, above described. In addition there were, at the commencement of the siege, placed in the fort two detachments, with their guns, from Captain Tobin's battery [1st Mississippi Light Artillery]. The embrasures were subsequently filled up, for reasons which will be hereafter stated. A flank on our left and another traverse were constructed for protection against a fire up the left valley. A ditch 2 feet deep was dug on the inside of the parapet, to enable the men to stand erect without being exposed to the enemy's fire. As the enemy's elongated shot traversed the parapet near its upper slope and killed several men, the parapet was strengthened by adding to its interior slope in some places 2 feet to its thickness. It was also found necessary to deepen the trenches and strengthen the breastworks of the rifle-pits on the right. I was also obliged to construct covered ways for the purpose of safe communication with the sinks and wells in the rear. And eventually it was deemed prudent to construct a strong line of rifle-pits across the gorge of the fort for the greater security of our rear, and to be used in case our lines should be breached or carried by assault. After all improvements, the interior of the fort was swept within 2 feet of the ground by the enemy's Minies. This did not prevent the men from bivouacking at night, lying flat on the ground; but during the day safety compelled them to seek the protection of the ditches next the parapet and traverses.

A Confederate countermine against the work known as A. J. Smith's Left Approach was fired on June 28, 1863. Two others were prepared but not fired. Both Federal sap rollers in front of the two approaches to this work were burned on July 1.

Railroad Redoubt (Fort Pettus or Beauregard)

Jutting out from the Confederate lines on a ridge 300ft above river level on the south side of the Alabama and Vicksburg Railroad cut, the Railroad Redoubt, also known as Fort Beauregard, may more accurately be described as a southeast-facing lunette with parallel flanks. Its parapet was about 24ft wide, including the superior and exterior slopes, and its ditch was 18ft wide and 7ft deep. Facing the Federal siege lines, its left flank consisted of an extended parapet with slight angle. This was dissected by two traverses, between which were posted two 12-pounders of Hudson's Mississippi Battery. A single 6-pounder of Waddell's Alabama Battery stood to their right. The left flank was composed of a shorter parapet, beyond which was a 6ft-deep trench extending from the ditch and connecting with the main line of Confederate rifle pits.

Defended by elements of the 30th Alabama and Waul's Texas Legion during May 1863, the rifle pits just to the south of the fort were defended by the 46th Alabama and the remainder of the 30th Alabama. The bulk of Waul's Legion acted as a reserve to shore up any breaks that occurred in the thinly defended works. A small redan to the south of the Railroad Redoubt, with a 16ft-wide parapet and 7ft-deep ditch, contained one 12-pounder of Vaiden's Mississippi Battery, and served as the daytime headquarters for Brigadier General S. D. Lee.

Also known as Fort Pettus or Fort Beauregard, the Railroad Redoubt was the only Confederate earthwork breached by Union forces on May 22, 1863. Stood by the tracks of the modern railroad, the scale of the site is still impressive today. (Courtesy of the National Park Service)

In this painting by Thure de Thulstrap, the 22nd Iowa are met by a hail of Minie balls and grenades as they struggle up the steep exterior slope of the Railroad Redoubt earthworks during the Union assault on May 22, 1863. (Library of Congress: LC-USZ62-12757)

The Railroad Redoubt was the only work breached by Union forces, consisting of elements of the 2nd Brigade, Tenth Division, 9th Army Corps, commanded by Colonel William J. Landrum, during the assault of May 22, 1863. According to the regimental history of the 48th Ohio:

> Landrum, on obtaining possession of the fort, put a pioneer force at work to throw up earth-works in the gorge, so as to bring the guns of the fort to bear upon the rebels ... The flags of the 48th Ohio, 77th Illinois and 19th Kentucky floated from the inner slope of the parapet from half-past 11 a.m. till 4 p.m. At the latter hour the rebels were seen preparing for a charge, to re-take the fort. An entire brigade was about to be pitted against a few companies. Our men did not receive the support which had been promised them, and were compelled to fall back, leaving the enemy again in possession of the fort.

In fact, only a small force of Confederate volunteers composed of 40 men of Waul's Texas Legion, led by Lieutenant Colonel E. W. Pettus, 20th Alabama Infantry, recaptured the redoubt. In his report of the action, General Stevenson recorded: "Undaunted, this little band, its chivalrous commander at its head, rushed upon the work, and in less time than it requires to describe it, it and the flags were in our possession. Preparations were then quickly made for the use of hand-grenades, when the enemy in the ditch, being informed of our purpose, immediately surrendered." Subsequent to the bravery of the Alabamian officer, the Railroad Redoubt was also referred to as Fort Pettus by the Confederates for the remainder of the siege.

Square Fort (Fort Garrott)

Controlling the southeast approaches to Vicksburg, the Square Fort was a four-sided redoubt which sat diagonally on the Confederate lines. The two faces projecting from the main line consisted of parapets about 26ft wide with ditches 8ft deep and 18ft wide. Those behind the lines were of the same dimensions minus the ditch.

According to General Alfred Cumming, commanding the Second Brigade of Stevenson's Division, his brigade moved into the Vicksburg trenches extending from the Square Fort to the Salient Work on May 18, 1863, where it remained "without relief for forty-seven days, until the capitulation of the city on July 4 ... No assault was made by the enemy along the brigade front during the continuation of the siege. An almost unremitting fire of sharpshooters was kept up during all hours of daylight during the whole time, varied by occasional brisk cannonading. The enemy's rifle-pits in time were so extended as to almost entirely envelop the brigade front, and were generally about 150 yards distant."

The Square Fort itself was garrisoned by elements of the 20th Alabama, commanded by Colonel Isham W. Garrott. This redoubt contained one 6-pounder and one 12-pounder howitzer, manned by Vaiden's Mississippi Battery, and another 12-pounder howitzer served by Waddell's Alabama Battery. Between June 16 and 17, 1863 the 20th Alabama suffered heavy casualties from the fire of Federal sharpshooters in rifle pits close to the fort. Exasperated by the damage being inflicted on his men, Garrott picked up a rifle-musket to help return fire and was shot through the heart. He died without learning that he had been promoted to brigadier general. The redoubt was subsequently named Fort Garrott in his honor.

The grass-covered parapets of the Square Fort, or Fort Garrott, today. The (bottom) aerial view shows how close the sap called Hovey's Approach was to the Confederate earthworks. (Courtesy of the National Park Service)

Salient Work (Horn Work)

Commanding the Hall's Ferry Road into Vicksburg, the Salient Work was so-called because of its advanced position in front of the general line, and consisted of an irregular redan with a short northerly face and a longer south face jutting out into no man's land, with an oblique angle at its end. Garrisoned by the two right flank companies of the 57th Georgia, commanded by Lieutenant Colonel Cincinnatus Guyton, and emplacing two guns, this work was not the object of a direct Federal attack during the 47-day siege. Two sorties were made from this work by its garrison, reinforced by the left companies of the 43rd Tennessee. During the second one, on the night of June 22, 1863, a lieutenant colonel and five enlisted men were captured, part of the Federal trench was filled in, and the next night a counter trench from the work was begun. The ground gained was held until the night of June 24, when it was taken by the enemy. A Confederate countermine against Lauman's Approach was prepared, but not fired.

South Fort

Anchoring the southernmost end of the Confederate lines to the Mississippi was South Fort. Originally part of Vicksburg's river defenses, the big guns mounted here at first could only register on the river. But provision was soon made so its ordnance could be quickly shifted to bear on Warrenton Road in the event the city was attacked from the landward side. The earthworks at this point consisted at its center and left of a series of redans linked together via a parapet, and a square bastion with open gorge at its right nearest the river. Garrisoned by the 40th Georgia Infantry, commanded by Lieutenant Colonel R. M. Young, it contained a 10in. columbiad and, for much of the siege, a 10in. mortar in its bastion, which continued to command the view of the river and the Federal naval approaches from the south. Two 6-pounder guns were placed in its center parapet. The former were the most powerful weapons in the land defenses around the city. The fort was manned by Tennessee and Georgia troops from the brigades of Colonel Alexander W. Reynolds and General Seth M. Barton. The columbiad and mortar were manned by Co. G, 1st Louisiana Heavy Artillery, while the 6-pounders were served by Co. A, 14th Mississippi Light Artillery.

The guns of Battery A (Chicago Light Artillery), 1st Illinois Light Artillery, commanded by Captain Peter P. Wood, stand behind a log breastwork with earthen traverses in front of the Confederate fortifications outside Vicksburg on May 22, 1863, four days after their arrival from Baker's Creek. The Stockade Redan is seen on the opposite ridge, with Vicksburg in the distance. (Author's collection)

The Union siege lines

Several hundred yards away from the Confederate position and roughly parallel to it was a ridge system not so continuous and more broken than that occupied by Pemberton's forces. Along this line the Union Army took position and, following its failure to breach the Confederate defenses from 18–22 May, 1863, began siege operations. The aggregate length of the Union siege lines was 12 miles, and by June 30, 1863 contained 89 batteries mounting 220 guns. Lacking a sufficient number of siege pieces, the Federals also had to rely on light guns to shell the Confederate defenses. The guns from those batteries in the rear were moved forward as the siege advanced. These batteries were sometimes constructed under the supervision of the pioneers of the division to which the battery belonged, and sometimes by the officer who was to command the finished work.

Due to a shortage of personnel, only three engineer officers were on duty on the Federal siege lines at Vicksburg at any one time. According to chief engineer Captain Frederick E. Prime:

> Over a line so extended and ground so rough as that which surrounds Vicksburg, only a general supervision was possible, and this gave to the siege one of its peculiar characteristics, namely, that many times, at different places, the work that should be done, and the way it should be done, depended on officers, or even on men, without either theoretical or practical knowledge of siege operations, and who had to rely upon their native good

During the night of June 13/14, 1863, Federal troops in a sap called "Ewing's Approach" crawled within 20 yards of the foot of the Stockade Redan and were attacked with hand-grenades and lighted shells by the garrison composed of the Mississippians and Missourians of Shoup's brigade. According to a Northern account of the incident, the Federals retaliated with their own grenades. In his battle report General F. A. Shoup commented: "Have organized my artillerists into a hand-grenade and thunder-barrel corps, since our guns are of no service." (Author's collection)

45

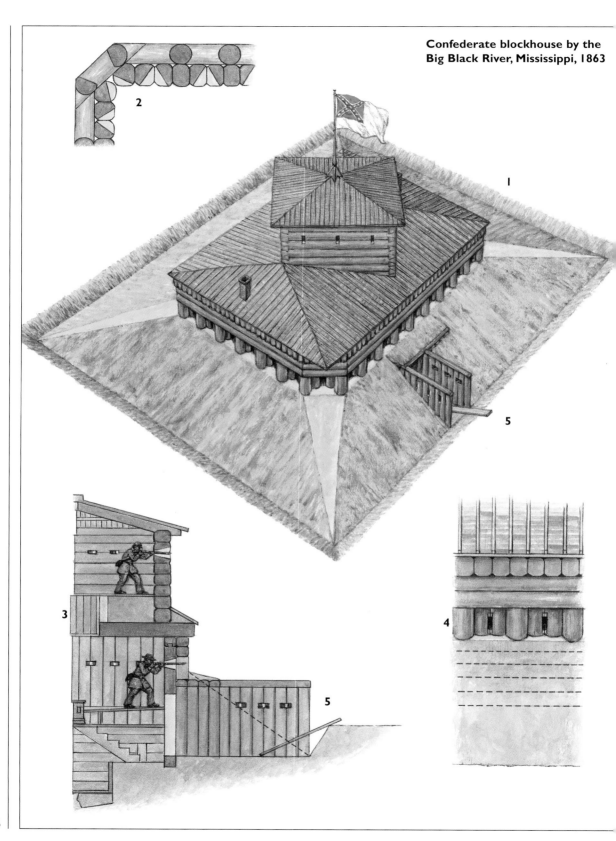

Confederate blockhouse by the Big Black River, Mississippi, 1863

The crew of the "Left piece" of Chicago Light Artillery etched their battle honors on its breech before turning their gun in. The honors read: "[Fort] Donelson, Shiloh, Vicksburg [meaning Chickasaw Bayou], Arkansas Post, Champion Hill, Vicksburg [meaning the siege]." It further notes: "Turned in June 1863 – fired 1,300 rounds." This gun stands today in the Vicksburg National Military Park Visitor Center. (Courtesy of the National Park Service)

sense and ingenuity. Whether a battery was to be constructed by men who had never built one before, a sap-roller made by those who had never heard the name, or a ship's gun-carriage to be built, it was done, and, after a few trials, was well done … The style of [larger works] was very varied, both reveting and platforms depending on the materials which could be obtained at the time. In some cases they were well and neatly reveted with gabions and fascines, and furnished with substantial plank platforms, while in others reveting of rough boards, [fence] rails, or cotton bales was used, and the platforms were made of boards and timber from the nearest barn or cotton-gin house. The larger part of the fascines, gabions, and sap-rollers was prepared by the pioneer companies of the different divisions.

Confederate blockhouse by the Big Black River, Mississippi, 1863

At the Battle of Big Black River Bridge during the Vicksburg campaign on May 16–17, 1863, Confederate forces recently defeated at Champion Hill, and consisting of three brigades under General John S. Bowen, manned a tête-de-pont consisting of two blockhouses plus rifle trenches guarding the railroad bridge at the railroad crossing of the Black River. Attacked by the Federal 2nd Brigade, Carr's Division, under General Michael K. Lawler, the Confederates were forced out of the trenches and blockhouses, and escaped across the river, at a loss of approximately 1,800 captured and 2,000 casualties. These troops would be sorely missed when the remains of Bowen's command withdrew into the Vicksburg defenses.

The main illustration (1) shows a two-story blockhouse with a double thickness of logs 18in. in diameter, with an outer layer of logs laid horizontally, and an inner layer stood vertically (2). The width recommended by Dennis Hart Mahan in his Treatise on Field Fortifications was 15ft, which theoretically allowed for a 6½ft-long "camp bed of boards" with a gap of 7ft in the middle, in which stood a stove. This also served as a banquette or firing platform for the garrison (3). Loopholes were set in the walls of both floors at intervals of 3ft (4). The upper floor was also provided with a banquette. For safety reasons, the magazine and stores were placed under the ground floor. Soil displaced from the surrounding ditch was banked against the outer walls to a height just below the loopholes. The entrance was masked by a double stockade (5), and access across the ditch was provided by a single plank, which was removed when necessary.

In his *Memoirs*, Grant stated:

> In no place were our lines more than six hundred yards from the enemy. It was necessary, therefore, to cover our men by something more than the ordinary parapet. To give additional protection sand bags, bullet-proof, were placed along the tops of the parapets far enough apart to make loopholes for musketry. On top of these, logs were put. By these means the men were enabled to walk about erect when off duty, without fear of annoyance from sharpshooters.

The batteries

At the northern end of the Union lines, Battery Selfridge was located opposite Fort Hill. Named for Lieutenant Commander Thomas O. Selfridge, Jr., the former commander of USS *Cairo*, an ironclad gunboat sunk by a mine in the Yazoo River on December 12, 1862, it was the only Federal battery which contained cannon manned exclusively by sailors. Detailed from Admiral David Dixon Porter's fleet, this battery served two 8in. Columbiads from June 5, 1863 until the end of the siege.

Established in front of the Stockade Redan, the Waterhouse Battery was commanded by Captain Allen C. Waterhouse, and was served by Battery E, 1st Illinois Light Artillery consisting of five guns. Next to this was Wood's Battery, composed of four guns manned by Battery A, 1st Illinois Light Artillery under Captain Peter P. Wood. Also in front of this part of the Confederate line was Battery Barrett, manned by Battery B, 1st Illinois Light Artillery commanded by Captain Samuel E. Barrett; Battery Hart under Captain Levi W. Hart, 8th Battery, Ohio Light Artillery; and Battery Jenney, named for Captain William L. B. Jenney, Acting Engineer Officer Fifteenth Army Corps.

The White House Battery was established on May 26, 1863 to the left of the Jackson Road, and in front of the Third Louisiana Redan. Named after the white-painted Shirley House nearby, it was constructed under the supervision of Captain

A Confederate shell explodes by the headquarters of Major General John A. Logan, commander of the 3rd Division, 17th Corps, in front of the 3rd Louisiana Redan in the Vicksburg lines. Gabions under construction are lined up by the bombproofs in which the troops are taking cover, while the tents have a screen of wood, known as blindage. (Author's collection)

Stewart R. Tresilian, engineer officer of the 3rd Division, 17th Army Corps, and contained four 24-pounder howitzers manned by Battery D, 1st Illinois Light Artillery, commanded by Captain Edward McAllister. Two of these guns were ordered forward to an advanced position at Battery Hickenlooper on June 6 until the end of the siege.

Established on June 4, 1863 as an advanced battery astride the Jackson Road, and less than 150 yards from the Third Louisiana Redan, Battery Hickenlooper was constructed under the direction of Captain Andrew Hickenlooper, chief engineer of Seventeenth Army Corps, on which occasion it was described as "irregular in shape, of 3,000 square feet, two embrasures on north and one on west face, and open to and covered by batteries in the rear." This battery eventually contained two 30-pounder Parrott rifles manned by the 1st US Infantry, one six-pounder served by the 3rd Battery Ohio Light Artillery, and 24-pounder howitzers manned by Co. D, 1st Illinois Light Artillery. The "Coonskin Tower" constructed for marksman Lieutenant Henry C. Foster stood to the left and rear of this work.

Named for Major General James B. McPherson, commanding the Seventeenth Army Corps, Battery McPherson was situated along the Jackson Road. Constructed by "a portion of the division pioneer corps" under the supervision of Captain Tresilian, it was described as "a sunken battery" and contained two 30-pounder Parrott rifles under Captain Robert H. Offley, 1st US Infantry. On June 11, these pieces were joined by two 9in. muzzle-loading Dahlgren guns, and the Parrott rifles were moved into an advanced battery eight days later. General Grant frequently visited this battery to watch the effect of its fire and that of the other batteries in sight. His favorite seat was on a certain log, which soon became known as his and was always reserved for him. With his guns under occasional heavy fire from the Twenty-first Louisiana Redan or Great Redoubt, Captain Offley was wounded on May 19, and his second in command, Lieutenant Charles Wilkins, was mortally wounded on May 25, 1863.

Located approximately one hundred yards south of Battery McPherson, Battery Logan contained six 10-pounder Parrott rifles from May 19 to June 22 manned by Battery M, 1st Missouri Light Artillery.

Directly opposite the Twenty-first Louisiana Redan, Battery De Golyer was one of the largest Federal positions. Named for Captain Samuel De Golyer, commander of the 8th Battery Michigan Light Artillery, who was mortally wounded by a stray bullet on May 28, 1863, it contained 20 guns which at various points in the siege consisted of two 12-pounder guns and two 3in. rifles served by the Independent Ohio Battery, commanded by Captain T. D. Yost; two 12-pounder howitzers and four James rifles, manned by the 8th Michigan Light Artillery; two 6-pounder guns and four James rifles worked by the 3rd Ohio Light Artillery; and four James rifles served by Battery L, 2nd Illinois Light Artillery. Three of these guns were moved to more forward positions during the course of the siege.

Established by Lieutenant Peter C. Haines, Chief Engineer Thirteenth Army Corps, on an elevation about 600 yards east of the Railroad Redoubt on May 20, 1863, Battery Maloney was also one of the more powerful in the Federal lines as it initially contained two 30-pounder and two 20-pounder Parrott rifles, commanded by Major Maurice Maloney, 1st US Infantry. Its caliber was increased later in the siege when two 8in. Dahlgren guns, procured from Admiral Porter's fleet, replaced the 20-pounders, which were moved closer to the Confederate lines.

At Battery Benton opposite South Fort, Acting Master J. Frank Reed of the gunboat USS *Benton* commanded two 42-pounder rifled guns taken off his vessel. These were manned by a detachment of Battery E, 1st Missouri Light Artillery, under Lieutenant Joseph B. Atwater, from the morning of July 1 to the end of the siege. On July 1 a shell exploded in the battery killing two and badly wounding four enlisted men of the 34th Iowa, who were serving as infantry support. All the remaining larger batteries between Batteries Maloney and Benton appear to have been given numbers rather than names, and numbered at least 18.

This recent photo of the sap in front of the Square Fort called Hovey's Left Approach illustrates how some of the trenches zigzagged as they approached the Confederate earthworks. (Courtesy of the National Park Service)

The saps

To bring the Union army close to the Confederate defense line, construction of protected approaches was begun. As the siege progressed saps, or approach trenches, 6ft deep and covered over in places by fascines, and screened by gabions, in order to conceal troops, zigzagged their way toward the works defending Vicksburg. Fourteen major approaches were carried forward by pick and shovel details, each connecting to a network of parallels, cavaliers, bombproofs, and artillery emplacements. These saps derived their names from the brigade or division commanders who furnished the guards and working parties. Thayer's Approach and Tunnel was established towards the Twenty-sixth Louisiana Redoubt. Giles A. Smith's Left and Right Approaches, Ewing's Approach and Buckland's Approach, with Lightburn's Approach stemming from the latter, were dug in front of the Stockade Redan. A. J. Smith's Left and Right Approaches invested the Second Texas Lunette. Carr's Left and Right Approaches threatened the Railroad Redoubt. Logan's Approach closed in on the 3rd Louisiana Redan from Battery Hickenlooper. Hovey's Approach neared the Square Fort, while Slack's Secondary Approach drew close to an angle in the trench line manned by the 23rd Alabama Infantry south of that fort. Herron's Approach invested the lines near South Fort.

The mines

The Federals dug mines under the Confederate lines and packed them with black powder. According to chief engineer Captain Frederick Prime, the "compactness of the alluvial soil" underneath the Vicksburg region made lining for mining galleries unnecessary. The Confederates tried unsuccessfully to stop them with numerous countermines. The first Federal mine was dug toward the Third Louisiana Redan, the tunnel of which was 3ft wide, 4ft high and 40ft long. On June 25, 1863 the Federals detonated (or "sprang") 2,200 lb. of explosives and blasted a crater 35ft wide by 12ft deep. A soldier in the 3rd Louisiana reported "Suddenly the earth under our feet gave a convulsive shudder and with a muffled roar, a mighty column of earth, men, poles, spades, and guns arose many feet in the air. About 50 lives were blotted out in that instant." Six Mississippians working in a countermine were buried alive in the earth thrown up by the blast. Two more mines were completed and several others begun during the siege.

Life in the Vicksburg fortifications

Both armies spent endless hours occupying the larger fortifications, plus trenches, rifle pits and shelters burrowed into hillsides known as "rat holes." In Grant's army, the digging and repair work was done by men of the pioneer companies of divisions, by details from troops manning the lines, or by free blacks. The latter were paid $10 a month and, according to Captain Frederick Prime, "proved to be very efficient laborers when under good supervision."

Regarding the troops in the Federal trenches in front of the Railroad Redoubt, an officer of the 48th Ohio Infantry recalled:

Our duty was to dig and man one of the rifle-pits, which was within one hundred yards of one of their main forts. To approach these rifle-pits, tunnels were made through the hills, thus connecting the ravines. The details for pickets and for digging rifle-pits, were always sent to their posts and relieved very quietly during the night. In some places we succeeded in digging the rifle-pits to within a few feet of their fort, being protected from their musketry by large bundles of cane [sap-rollers], that were kept in front while approaching, the enemy in the meantime trying to get possession of the cane by means of hooks attached to long poles, or destroying them by throwing turpentine-balls and setting them on fire, while our men in return would annoy them by throwing hand grenades and short-fuse shells into their fort, which usually elicited quite a spirited conversation between the combatants.

As the Union saps came closer to the Confederate works, sharpshooters on both sides gained better opportunities to pick off enemy soldiers. A letter dated June 10, 1863 from an unknown member of the 76th Illinois Infantry, which was part of Lauman's Division opposite the Salient Work, reported in the Newark *True American*: "A portion of the regiment is kept in the rifle-pits with reliefs every two hours, and they are getting the range on the butternuts so well that when one raises his head to fire, half a dozen balls from our Springfields raise the dust on top of the rifle pits so close to him that he is soon silenced."

Part of Sherman's Corps on the extreme right of the Union lines, Private Adoniram J. Withrow, 25th Iowa Infantry, wrote on June 3, 1863 that his regiment had been "digging Rifle Pits, and moving closer until our right is within fifty yards of one of the principal Water Bataries [sic], and they can in a great measure keep stuck silenced[.] Yesterday morning Jo Campbell and some more of the boys were in a new pit that had been dug the night before, & of which the rebs had no knowledge, when out came four or five rebs out of their tents and were putting on their cloths [sic]. Jo took deliberate aim and there was one rebel less to contend against."

As a result of the limited number of effective Confederate troops available to General Pemberton in the Vicksburg defenses, every man fit for duty had to be placed in the trenches and rifle-pits, and remained there, enduring sun, rain, mud, poor food, plus the shells and bullets of the Federal army. The unending barrage of small arms and artillery fire, one Confederate exclaimed, could be compared to men clearing land – the report of musketry is like the chopping of axes and that of the cannon like the felling of trees." To defend against surprise night attacks, they were forced to sleep on their arms in the trenches.

With a shortage of ammunition, the Confederates had to be economic with its use. According to Captain A. C. Roberts, 23rd Alabama Infantry, in the Square Fort: "The fire from our trenches upon the enemy was slow and deliberate.

The sharpshooters

Renowned as a "fine shot," Lieutenant Colonel William E. Strong, an officer of the 12th Wisconsin Infantry on the staff of General J. B. McPherson, is shown here among Federal sharpshooters in a rifle trench in the Vicksburg siege lines. Based on an original sketch by Theodore R. Davis, this engraving was published in *Harper's Weekly* on June 27, 1863 with the following account: "The sketch is of an incident coming under my observation while, a few days since, I was making my way, with due regard for personal safety, through the trenches and rifle-pits to a point from which a near view of the rebel works could be obtained. An officer of General M'Pherson's staff, a fine shot, had taken his rifle, and was, with the sharp-shooters, rendering it an impossibility to use a gun that had been used to annoy our men at work in the trenches. A sharp-shooter from the rebel works was crawling, as he thought, unseen, to a point nearer our line. A hat placed invitingly was, in a few moments, shot through by the ball from his rifle. The moment was the rebel's last: he had exposed his head in shooting. And the sharp-shooting officer now wears an airy hat. I am told by a deserter that seventeen men have been shot from a spot called by them 'The Dead Hole.'" (Author's collection)

We did not waste our powder, but no Abolitionist could show his head without danger from ball or buck-shot. The necessity for constant watchfulness made the sentinel duty at night heavy and wearing." A correspondent for the Mobile *Tribune* reported how a one-eyed Confederate sharpshooter in the 30th Alabama called Elliott caused havoc among the ranks of the Union army from behind the parapets at the Square Fort: "he shoots a Belgian rifle, whenever the peculiar whistle of that weapon is heard the Yankees call out, 'Look out, boys, there's old One Eye!' They say he can kill at one thousand yards, and never misses. One day two Yankee Captains were looking from behind a cotton bale, and old One Eye killed them both with one shot." The report concluded that Elliott was known in Alabama as "the best marksman in the state."

In the Union lines opposite the Third Louisiana Redan was Lieutenant Henry C. Foster, Co. B, 23rd Indiana Infantry, a celebrated marksman who wore a distinctive cap of raccoon fur that earned him the nickname "Coonskin." Loaded with provisions, Foster would creep close to the Confederate lines at night, where he constructed a burrow with a peephole in it. Remaining in his hideout for hours at a time, he sniped at the Confederate defenders. Foster took things a step further when he constructed a log tower armored with railroad iron and cross-ties from the destroyed Jackson and Vicksburg Railroad that provided a clearer view inside the enemy lines. Using what became known as the "Coonskin Tower" as a sheltered firing platform, he placed a mirror at the upper, back portion of the tower and positioned it at a slight angle to enable him to see inside the Confederate works. All day long he crouched behind railroad ties staring at the mirror. Whenever anyone came into view, he stood, quickly fired, and then ducked down behind shelter in case a Confederate returned fire. In this manner he was able to conduct his activities with virtual impunity.

According to Private Jefferson Moses, Co. G, 93rd Illinois Infantry, whose regiment occupied the trenches in front of the Railroad Redoubt: "When I got to the company and could go out and look over and see the rebels forts I thought it just fun. Our company was out on picket. One day we had to lay in rifel [sic] pits about three feet wide, three or more deep. I know I got awful tired so I got up and set on the ground that was taken out of the ditch. I did not set long till the Captain seen me. He yelled out get down there. You will get your head shot off. I just droped [sic] down when zip came a bullet. To say I was scared is mild. I never after that exposed myself."

For protection against artillery fire, the troops in both armies dug shelters in the reverse slope of their defense works. Reinforced with heavy timbers, they afforded some protection from enemy fire. In the Confederate ranks, Corporal

Ephraim M. Anderson, Co. G, 2nd Missouri Infantry, whose brigade was held in reserve and often relieved the Louisianians, described these "rat holes" as follows:

> When stopping for several days at the same place, we were accustomed to dig holes to sleep in during the night, and generally had a blanket stretched over, or a covering of cane, bark, or anything else that was suitable and convenient to keep the sun out in the day. They were easily made by cutting down about two feet in to the side of a hill and throwing off to a level below, which made an even and smooth surface to lie upon, somewhat more protected and decidedly more comfortable than the natural face of the ground. As the siege progressed, it became so that we could find these holes almost every place to which we were ordered, and were spared the trouble of constructing them.

Inclement weather combined with long hot days caused further problems for the men occupying the rifle pits. Lieutenant Jared Sanders II, Co. B, 26th Louisiana, recorded in his diary on June 17, 1863: "Made a place to get into during rain by covering 12 feet of pits with wood covered with dirt. Have my bed inside of the ditch." On June 1, Sergeant William H. Tunnard, Co. K, 3rd Louisiana Infantry, wrote that it was a "clear and unusually warm day. The men sought shelter from the sun's scorching rays beneath the shade of out-stretched blankets, and in small excavations and huts in the hill sides."

To prevent surprise attacks, both armies posted pickets in advance of their lines at night. With the lines so close in the latter stages of the siege, pickets would often stand within a few feet of one another, or even side by side. The report of captains Prime and Comstock, chief engineer officers of the Federal Army of the Tennessee, stated on November 29, 1863: "On one occasion, in front of [Major General E. O. C.] Ord's [Thirteenth Army] corps, our pickets, in being posted, became intermixed with the enemy's, and after some discussion the opposing picket officers arranged their picket lines by mutual compromise, these lines in places not being more than 10 yards apart." Discussions of good shots and bad officers, or vice versa, helped to pass the long night watches. By common agreement, out of respect for the exposed and unprotected position of the sentinels, there was generally no firing at men on picket duty. Lieutenant Lewis Guion, Co. D, 26th Louisiana Infantry, recorded in his diary on June 21, 1863, that there was "friendly feeling between men [in] pits by redan[.] Yankees exchanging rations giving boxes of sardines, coffee, paper &c."

Providing 17 Confederate and 22 Union regiments, Missouri was heavily represented in both armies during the siege. One day the pickets at the Stockade Redan, which was heavily garrisoned by Missourians, agreed to informal short truces. Called the "Trysting Place," the area became a meeting ground for relatives or friends of the Missouri troops of both sides.

The "Coonskin Tower" was made of thick railroad ties, which provided ample protection from Confederate rifle fire. By the time the tower was constructed, Union batteries and sharpshooters were firmly in control of the area, and prevented the Confederates from firing on it when Lieutenant Foster was in residence. (Courtesy of National Park Service)

Battery Hickenlooper during the siege of Vicksburg

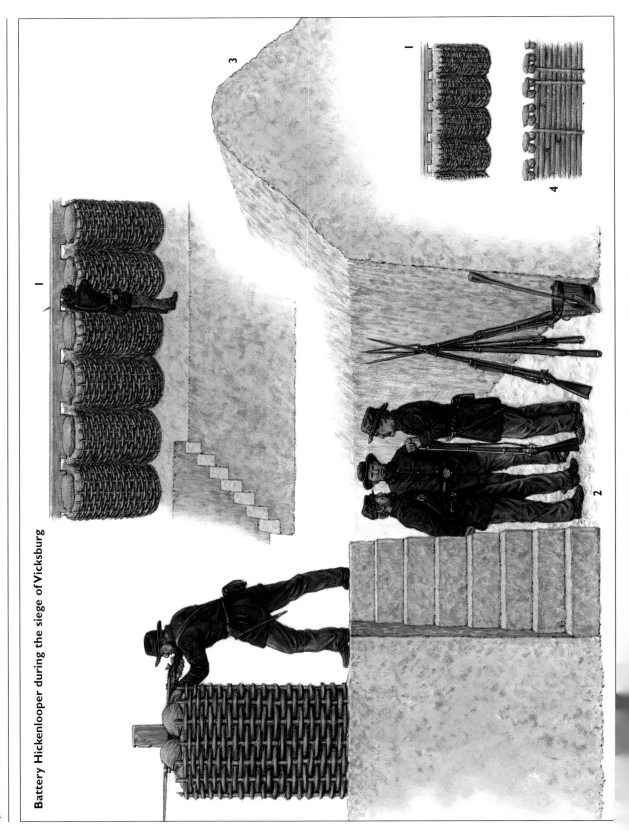

While available, Confederate rations were generally prepared by details of soldiers behind the lines and carried to the troops at the breastworks. On June 4, 1863, Sergeant Tunnard, 3rd Louisiana, recorded: "The ration furnished each man was: peas, one-third of a pound; meal, two-thirds of five-sixths of a pound; beef, one-half of a pound, including in the weight bones and shanks; sugar, lard, soup, and salt in like proportions ... To the perils of the siege began now to be added the prospect of famine." By June 23, Lieutenant Sanders, 26th Louisiana wrote: "Rations are short & we eat two meals per day at 9 in morning & at 3 in evening – stylish in a ditch!" The ultimate cause of the Confederate surrender, food supplies eventually ran out and the defenders were forced to scavenge for food. According to Major Lockett: "We were short of provisions, so that our men had been on quarter rations for days before the close of the siege; had eaten mule meat, and rats, and young shoots of cane, with the relish of epicures dining on the finest delicacies of the table."

The overall impact of the siege of Vicksburg on Confederate troops is best summarized by Private William P. Chambers, Co. H, 37th Mississippi Infantry:

And so the days wore on – each one almost a repetition of the one that preceded it. The long, hot, dreary days, and nights of toil and danger were telling on the men. Emaciated by hunger, worn out by constant watching and utterly sceptical as to any promised hopes of relief, their despondency deepened, and they felt more keenly than ever, how useless it was to prolong the struggle. They heard no sound from one sunrise till the next save the crack of the rifle, the boom of the cannon, the screech of the shells and the "whizz" of bullets.

Protected by a gabion revetment, Union sharpshooters line the banquette tread in this flying sap constructed by Captain Hickenlooper for Logan's Division in front of the Third Louisiana Redan in the Vicksburg siege lines. The "Coonskin Tower" constructed by marksman Lieutenant Henry C. Foster is seen at rear right. (Author's collection)

Battery Hickenlooper during the siege of Vicksburg

Construction of the Federal flying sap and trench near Battery Hickenlooper, and in front of the Third Louisiana Redan, at Vicksburg, was completed under the direction of Captain Andrew Hickenlooper, chief engineer of the Union Seventeenth Army Corps. The flying sap was composed of soil-filled gabions with a double-thickness of sandbags placed on top with gaps between for loopholes. On top of this notched wooden logs were laid, which enabled the men to stand up to full height without presenting a target for Confederate sharpshooters (1). Steps cut in the bank led to a 6ft-deep trench below, where reserve troops rested and recovered before taking their turn back on the firing line (2). Soil piled to the rear of the trench formed a parados, or protection against rear attack and flying shell fragments (3). The Confederate breastworks at Vicksburg generally consisted of sand-bagged loopholes and log revetments (4).

The fate of the fortifications

Little remains today of the forts and earthworks that played such a vital role in operations along the Mississippi and other rivers during the Civil War. Built as temporary fortifications from earth and wood, and using sod, cotton, and gabions made from locally grown cane for revetment, they quickly eroded or disappeared under water as river levels changed during the years following the Civil War.

When the Tennessee River was dammed as part of the Tennessee Valley Authority project in the late 1930s creating Kentucky Lake, what remained of Fort Henry was submerged forever. A small navigation beacon marks the location of the northwest corner of the former fortification. The site is today managed by the US Forest Service as a part of the "Land between the Lakes National Recreation Area." However, across the river the remains of Fort Heiman survive in woodlands and retain much of their original historic character, including earthwork fortifications, outer trench lines, an upper battery or fortified redoubt, and a possible powder magazine. Fort Heiman was added to the National Register of Historic Places on December 12, 1976, but remained on privately owned land until October 30, 2006, when 150 acres associated with the site was transferred to the National Park Service of the United States Department of the Interior for management as part of the Fort Donelson National Battlefield. Regarding the latter, the Park Service established Fort Donelson National Military Park and National Cemetery on March 26, 1928. This site was transferred from the War Department to the National Park Service on August 10, 1933, and was listed on the National Register on October 15, 1966. It was re-designated a National Battlefield on August 16, 1985.

Of Island No. 10, today there remains little sign. By 1883, it had become almost completely submerged. In his novel *Life on the Mississippi* published that year, Mark Twain stated: "I found the river greatly changed at Island No. 10. The

Photographed in February 2006, three 32-pounder guns on barbette carriages overlooking the Cumberland River indicate the position of part of the nine-gun lower water battery at Fort Donelson in 1862. (Photograph courtesy of Hal Jespersen)

Photographed within the Confederate defenses after the fall of Port Hudson on July 9, 1863, a Confederate siege gun on wooden casemate carriage lies destroyed in the foreground, while wooden barrels filled with soil form a gabion revetment topped with sandbags in the parapet. (US Army Military History Institute)

island which I remembered was some three miles long and a quarter of a mile wide, heavily timbered, and lay near the Kentucky shore – within two hundred yards of it, I should say. Now, however, one had to hunt for it with a spy-glass. Nothing was left of it but an insignificant little tuft, and this was no longer near the Kentucky shore; it was clear over against the opposite shore, a mile away."

Much of the remains of Fort Pillow were also eroded away as the Arkansas River changed its course during the post-Civil War years. Fort Pillow State Park was established in 1929, and was transferred to Federal control and designated a national memorial in 1964. An outline of the rifle-pits and trenches that extended from the salient angle of the northwestern bastion of the fort is still visible, and the story of the fort is told at the Arkansas Post National Memorial visitor center and via several site markers.

In May 1962, the Grand Gulf Military Monument Park, near Port Gibson, Mississippi, was officially opened. This 400-acre site preserves the earthwork remains of Forts Cobun and Wade. Excavation of the powder magazine at Fort Wade began in 1977, and the Grand Gulf Military State Park Museum at Port Gibson contains artifacts and history appertaining to both sites. Some of the earthworks at Port Hudson remain relatively unspoiled, although new housing developments and utility lines are damaging many features today. In May 1974, both the battlefield and cemetery were designated a National Historic Landmark by the US Department of the Interior.

One of the five original national parks established in 1899, Vicksburg National Military Park preserves the site of the siege of Vicksburg. Initially placed under the jurisdiction of the War Department, it was transferred to the National Park Service in 1933. The park consists generally of the Confederate and Union siege lines, now indicated by Confederate and Union Avenues and the area between. The park's 30 miles of avenues and about 1,330 acres of federally owned land contain 128 artillery pieces and 1,600 monuments, markers, and tablets, as well as 17 state memorials.

Glossary

Abatis Consisting of felled trees stripped of their leaves and smaller branches with remaining branches sharpened into points and placed side by side, abatis were used extensively in front of the Confederate defenses at Vicksburg. Usually positioned on the glacis, or outer slope of field fortifications exterior to the ditch, their purpose was to break the momentum of an assaulting body of troops and hold them up under close musket fire delivered from the parapet.

Boyaux Communication trenches providing covered ways between and along parallels and from parallels to batteries were known as boyaux. Those for infantry were usually wide enough for the passage of two men, although dimensions could be increased when it was necessary to pass artillery through the trenches rather than move guns and howitzers into position over open ground under cover of darkness. Commanding the troops in the Twenty-sixth Louisiana Redoubt at Vicksburg, General Francis A. Shoup recalled that the Federals "constructed a covered way parallel to the stockade by digging a deep ditch and covering it with fence rails, two or three deep, to prevent us throwing hand grenades and other destructive missiles and explosives over upon them."

Breastworks Any protective embankment for infantry was commonly termed a breastwork. These were mostly formed from logs, fence rails, or rocks. Sandbags were often used to repair breaches in breastworks. However, with a glut of cotton languishing on Southern quaysides due to the cotton embargo imposed by the Confederacy in an attempt to gain international recognition, cotton bales were often used for the same purpose. One of its first recorded uses was at Memphis, Tennessee, where the city authorities were alarmed at the build up of Union forces at Cairo, Illinois and feared a possible Northern "raid" down river. On June 11, 1861, the *Weekly Journal* of Louisville, Kentucky, commented: "The people [of Memphis] … have been hauling out two thousand bales of cotton for breastworks, expecting Cairo to be along any day." Five days earlier, the Memphis *Daily Appeal* had reported: "The bluff is to be protected by breastworks of cotton. Yesterday, the bluff, between Court and Adams streets, was thus lined with bales. Each of the streets in the city, with the exception of Madison and Jefferson, is to be thus barricaded. The superintendence of the construction of these defences, has been entrusted by Gen. Pillow to Messrs. E. M. Apperson and John Martin, Esq. With breastworks on the bluff, and breastworks in the streets, Memphis will be in war trim."
The Union army also utilized cotton bales in its fortifications. Responsible for the construction of the Union siege works at Port Hudson, Louisiana in 1863, engineer officer Major Joseph M. Bailey ordered a cotton-bale fortress known as "Battery Bailey" or the "Great Cotton Bale Battery" to be built opposite the Confederate fortifications called the "Citadel." Completed by June 26, its guns played a crucial role in the remaining siege operations.

Cavaliers A cavalier was a trench with its parapet raised high enough to see over the crest of the glacis and command a fortification's field of fire. Responsible for the siege works in front of the Stockade Redan at Vicksburg, Acting Engineer Officer Captain William Kossak reported that, on June 20–21, 1863, he tried to "raise trench cavaliers parallel to enemy's counterscarp and get a plunging fire into his ditch." Leaving a sap roller in position, he crowned it with gabions and sandbags, so as to "offer the pickets supporting [the] working party a proper shelter."

Fascines Constructed from brushwood and filled with soil to serve as revetment material in field works, fascines during the siege of Vicksburg were made from cane, which grew in abundance in the area.

Flying saps A flying sap was a trench with soil-filled gabions placed along its engaged side, which served as a breastwork. Such siege works were always constructed under cover of darkness with infantry support to protect the working party against sorties by the garrison.

Gabions A gabion consisted of a cylindrical wicker basket filled with soil, and was used to retain the sides and slopes of earthworks. Gabion revetments were created by placing a number of gabions side by side, and extra height could be gained by placing fascines on top as the foundation for another row of gabions. According to Captain Frederick E. Prime, Chief Engineer, Union Army of the Tennessee, during the siege of Vicksburg: "Material for the wattling of gabions was abundant, grape-vines being chiefly used, though these made gabions that were inconveniently heavy, from the fact that vines of too large size were taken. Captain Freeman, aide-de-camp, experimented with cane as material for wattling, and found by crushing the joints with a mallet the rest of the cane was split sufficiently to allow it to be woven between the stakes of the gabion and yet be strong, making a good and very neat gabion."

Gorge Field fortifications consisting of redans and lunettes were usually not protected by a rear parapet. According to some schools of thought, this permitted the defending force to make a rapid withdrawal if overrun. It also made it easier to re-take the position, if undertaken before the attacking force had time to throw up breastworks.

Unused gabions waiting their soil filling are seen near the Union mine works in front of the Third Louisiana Redan at Vicksburg in this engraving, as *Frank Leslie's Illustrated* artist Fred B. Schell sketches the scene. (Author's collection)

Lunette In field fortification a lunette was a detached field work open at the gorge, and traced with two faces forming a salient angle and two flanks adjoining the faces. The Twenty-seventh Louisiana and Second Texas lunettes in the Vicksburg defenses were both irregular in shape.

Parallel Siege works used to provide defensive positions allowing the besieging army to hold the ground gained by its saps, or approaches, were called parallels. These were laid out either parallel to the point of attack, or on a concentric line that enveloped it. As the sap advanced, the parallels were also used as forward supply depots where siege materials necessary to complete the trenches in front were gathered.

Redan More commonly used in the Western theater of operations, a redan was a simple field work consisting of two faces joined to form a salient angle. This basic shape, or trace, could be modified by adding auxiliary flanks or creating double, or even triple, redans.

Revetment The facing wall of earthworks and field fortifications was known as the revetment. Where materials were available, this usually consisted of wicker gabions filled with soil. Otherwise, wooden barrels or cotton bales were employed. Revetments were sometimes unnecessary in the Vicksburg lines due to the compactness of the alluvial soil in that locality. According to the report of captains Prime and Comstock, chief engineer officers of the Federal Army of the Tennessee, dated November 29, 1863: "In close approaches the sap was reveted with gabions, empty barrels, or with cotton bales, or sometimes left unreveted, it being difficult to prevent the working parties from sinking the sap to the depth of 5 or even 6 feet when the enemy's fire was heavy, and reveting then was unnecessary."

Rifle loop-holes Loop-holes were inserted into fortification breastworks to enable sharpshooters in both armies to fire without exposing themselves to the enemy. These were sometimes created using head-logs, which involved a log resting on blocks or skids being placed along the crest of the parapet. The riflemen used the slit created underneath through which to fire their weapons. The skids also served to catch the log if struck by artillery, and sent it rolling backwards over the heads of the men in the trench. Loopholes were also formed by placing two sandbags a few inches apart on the parapet. This method was employed by the Confederates in their Vicksburg defenses. Placed on top of breastworks, moveable wooden logs or boards with as many as five loopholes cut through were also used by the Union army at Vicksburg.

Sandbags Measuring about 32in. long and 14in. wide when empty, and 27in. long by nine inches in diameter when filled and tied, sandbags provided a good form of revetment when field fortifications were required quickly, or the soil was very thin and unsuited to the formation of a sound parapet. An effective sandbag revetment was created by placing the courses of sandbags alternate ways, creating headers and stretchers. Confederate fortification surrounding Vicksburg was revetted with sandbags since plank wood was difficult to obtain in the immediate area, and much of the ground along the water front consisted of marshland. The canvas cloth used to make the sandbags consisted of tent-flies and old tents.

Sap rollers A sap roller was a bulletproof, moveable field fortification rolled on its side at the head of a sap to protect the sappers advancing the trench from enemy fire. Sap rollers generally consisted of a larger, gabion-style,

The ordnance store at Fort Henry was a log-built structure with shingled lean-to roof. The detail in this *Harper's Weekly* engraving indicates the roof was also covered with soil for additional protection and fireproofing. (Author's collection)

cylindrical, woven cane basket about 4½ft in diameter and 7ft in length, with a smaller basket placed inside it and packed out with fascines, earth, or cotton. At Vicksburg, Federal sappers in Hovey's Approach experienced difficulty making sap rollers that were impervious to Minie balls and not too heavy for use on the rough ground over which the saps ran. According to engineer officer Frederick E. Prime: "The difficulty was obviated by Lieutenant [P. C.] Hains, engineers, who caused two barrels to be placed head to head and secured, and the sap-roller to be built up of cane fascines around this hollow core."

Terreplein A terreplein was a level area immediately in the rear of the parapet of a redoubt, redan, or lunette.

Têtes-de-pont Fortifications that offered protection to a bridge or river crossing were called têtes-de-pont, and were employed at several points during the Vicksburg campaign.

Traverse A traverse was a raised barrier designed to defilade, or obscure from the view of the enemy, the interior spaces of a field work. A battery traverse was placed in batteries between guns to limit the damage caused by the explosion of an enemy shell on the work. Parados traverses were positioned independently of the parapet and across the terreplein, or parade, of an enclosed field work. Although usually made of earth with gabion revetment, other materials are known to have been used. A defilade traverse of cotton bales was erected on July 1, 1863 to protect from flanking fire a Federal sap called Slack's Secondary Approach near Fort Garrott during the siege of Vicksburg.

Trenches and rifle-pits Under fire Civil War units could quickly dig trenches and rifle-pits, even when not in possession of appropriate digging implements. When the Federal attack on the Vicksburg defenses began on May 18, 1863, the 26th Louisiana Infantry, under Colonel Winchester Hall, was ordered to withdraw from an advanced line of rifle-pits in front of the Stockade Redan, and found themselves "almost without intrenchments." According to the report of their brigade commander, General Shoup: "Few tools could be had, but in a surprisingly short time a very tolerable cover was constructed."

Trous-de-loup Consisting of deep pits dug just beyond the crest of the counterscarp, trous-de-loup often had sharpened stakes planted at their bottom to impale an unsuspecting enemy unfortunate enough to fall into them Lieutenant Joseph Dixon, CS Army, had them added to the southern approaches of Fort Donelson during November, 1861, and reported that small trees had been dragged "over the open space" in order to surprise an attacking force.

Wire entanglements First reported in use in the Eastern theater of the war by the Confederate army in the Shenandoah Valley in May, 1863 (see Fortress 38: *American Civil War Fortifications (2) Land and field fortifications*, p. 25), "entanglements of pickets and telegraph wire" were included as "obstructions in front of exposed points" in the Confederate defenses at Vicksburg on the 25th of the same month.

Visiting the forts today

The following selection is not exhaustive, but includes the main historical sites containing fortifications owned by the National Park Service, government agencies, the local community, plus those in private hands. At the time of writing all of these sites are open to the public unless otherwise noted.

Fort D at Cape Girardeau

Fort D at Cape Girardeau was purchased by the local chapter of the American Legion in 1936 with a view to preservation. Of the numerous earthen Civil War forts that once existed in the state, this is believed to the lone survivor. Today it forms part of a three-acre municipal park owned by the city of Cape Girardeau, and there are plans to re-establish an interpretation trail at the site.
Location: Cape Girardeau, Missouri.
Owner: American Legion.

Fort Henry

Fort Henry is now mostly underwater in Kentucky Lake.
Location: "Land Between the Lakes Recreation Area," west of Dover, Tennessee.
Owner: US Forest Service.

Fort Donelson National Battlefield

Fort Donelson National Battlefield contains restored earthworks including the Water Battery, Jackson's Battery, French's Battery, and Maney's Battery. The Union built a second earthwork fort nearby in 1863, and this site is now the National Cemetery.
Location: Near Dover, Tennessee.
Owner: National Park Service.
Website: www.nps.gov/fodo

Fort Pillow State Historic Park

Fort Pillow State Historic Park consists of 1,642 acres, which include extensive remains of earthworks, plus a reconstructed main redoubt and an Interpretive Center/Museum.
Location: Near Henning, Tennessee.
Website: tennessee.gov/environment/parks/FortPillow

Arkansas Post (Fort Hindman)

Arkansas Post (Fort Hindman) vanished beneath the water as the Arkansas River ate away the bluff on which the site stood as it changed course during the years following the Civil War. The Arkansas Post National Memorial Visitor Center offers a brief history and interpretation of the attack on the fort. Remains of the rifle-pits and trenches that extended from the salient angle of the northwestern bastion of the fort are still visible, and an account of the attack on the fort is offered at the Park Service visitor center.
Location: Near Gillett, Arkansas.
Website: www.nps.gov/arpo

Fort Pemberton

Fort Pemberton is included in the Fort Pemberton Park where some of the original breastworks may be found. The Cottonlandia Museum at Greenwood contains a cannon used in the defense of Fort Pemberton in March 1863.
Location: Near Greenwood, Mississippi.

After surviving bombardment by heavy 20-pounder Parrott rifles, "Fort Desperate" at Port Hudson lay in ruins on July 9, 1863. A smashed Confederate siege gun on wooden casemate carriage lies destroyed on the remains of its platform in the foreground. The horizontal slats of wood in the background appear to comprise the cover for a dugout where the Confederate troops sought refuge from the Union artillery. At right and in the rear is the main parapet of the redoubt. (National Archives)

Grand Gulf Military Monument Park
Forts Cobun and Wade are preserved within the Grand Gulf Military Monument Park. Remains include earthworks on both sites, plus an excavated powder magazine at Fort Wade.
Location: Near Port Gibson, Mississippi.
Website: www.grandgulfpark.state.ms.us

Camp Parapet
Camp Parapet is all that remains of the "Parapet line" in New Orleans. All that survives is the powder magazine, a brick structure encased in a mound of earth. It is fenced in, surrounded by residences, but is available for visits and tours by appointment only, by contacting the Jefferson Parish volunteer curator.
Location: Jefferson Parish, New Orleans, Louisiana.

Port Hudson State Historic Site
Port Hudson State Historic Site encompasses 650 acres of the northern portion of the Port Hudson battlefield, and contains extensive remains of earthworks and trenches, three observation towers, six miles of trails, and a museum. Four thousand Civil War veterans are buried at the Port Hudson National Cemetery, which stands just outside the old Confederate lines.
Location: Port Hudson, Louisiana.
Owner: Louisiana Department of Culture, Recreation, and Tourism.
Website: tps.cr.nps.gov/nhl/detail.cfm?ResourceId=1440&ResourceType=Site

Vicksburg National Military Park
Vicksburg National Military Park includes extensive earthwork remains, 1,330 monuments and markers, a 16-mile tour road, a restored Union gunboat, and a National Cemetery. The Interpretive Center and Museum contains exhibits explaining and illustrating the Vicksburg operations, and has an electrical relief map synchronized with a recorded lecture which offers a full explanation of the campaign and siege.
Location: Vicksburg, Mississippi.
Owner: National Park Service.
Website: www.nps.gov/vick

Bibliography and further reading

Ambrose, Stephen E. *Struggle for Vicksburg* (Eastern Acorn Press, 1982).

Arnold, James R. *Grant Wins the War: Decision at Vicksburg* (New York: John Wiley, 1997).

Ballard, Michael B. *The Campaign for Vicksburg* (Eastern National Park & Monument Association, 1996).

Bearss, Edwin C. *The Vicksburg Campaign*. 3 vols. (Dayton, OH: Momingside House, 1985–86).

Bering, John A. and Montgomery, Thomas *History of the 48th Ohio Veteran Volunteer Infantry* (Hillsboro, OH, 1880).

Carter, Samuel III *The Final Fortress: The Campaign for Vicksburg 1862–1863* (New York: St. Martin's Press, 1980).

Cimprich, John *Fort Pillow, a Civil War Massacre, and Public Memory* (Baton Rouge, LA: 2005).

Eisterhold, John A. "Fort Heiman [on the Tennessee River in the state of Tennessee]: Forgotten Fortress," *West Tennessee Historical Society's Papers*, 28 (1974).

Foote, Shelby *The Beleaguered City: The Vicksburg Campaign* (New York: The Modern Library, 1995).

Grabau, Warren E. *Ninety-Eight Days: A Geographer's View of the Vicksburg Campaign* (Knoxville, TN: University of Tennessee Press, 2000).

Hankinson, Alan *Vicksburg 1863* (Campaign 26: Osprey Publishing, Oxford, 1993).

Lockett, Samuel "The Defense of Vicksburg," *Battles & Leaders of the Civil War*, Vol. III (New York, 1956).

Richard, Allan C. Jr. and Higginbotham Richard, Mary Margaret *The Defense of Vicksburg* (College Station, TX: 2004).

Scott, Robert N. *The War of the Rebellion: A Compilation of the Official Records of the Union: and Confederate Armies* (Washington, DC: 1880–1901).

Shea, William L. and Winschel, Terrence J. *Vicksburg is the Key: The Struggle for the Mississippi* (Lincoln: University of Nebraska Press, 2003).

Wright, Howard C. *Port Hudson: its History from an Interior Point of View* (St. Francisville, LA, 1937).

Photographed after capture on July 9, 1863, one of the Confederate redoubts defending Port Hudson, Louisiana, sits atop a craggy 80ft bluff overlooking the Mississippi River. (US Army Military History Institute)

Index